Brand Conscious ENTREPRENEURS

A brand isn't born... it's created

Brand Conscious ENTREPRENEURS

A brand isn't born... it's created

AJAY ADLAKHA

Worldwide Published by
Pendown Press

PENDOWN PRESS
An ISO 9001 & ISO 14001 Certified Co.,
Regd. Office: 2525/193, 1st Floor, Onkar Nagar-A,
Tri Nagar, Delhi-110035
Ph.: 09350849407, 09312235086
E-mail: info@pendownpress.com
Branch Office: 1A/2A, 20, Hari Sadan, Ansari Road,
Daryaganj, New Delhi-110002
Ph.: 011-45794768
Website: PendownPress.com

First Edition: 2023

ISBN: 978-93-5554-315-8

Printed and Bound in India by Thomson Press India Ltd.

*Dedicated to thousands of
entrepreneurs who are struggling to
develop a legacy brand.*

Contents

About the author

Ajay Adlakha, Managing director, Infinity Advertising services, is an engineer by education and a passionate Entrepreneur-cum-Marketer by profession. He has expertise in Retail, Rural, and Branding, helping business owners to look at these three aspects while building their brands. A veteran of more than 2 decades in Brand Advisory and Integrated Marketing Communications, Ajay is an alumni of IIM Bangalore (Strategic Management) & MICA (Management Program). His expertise ranges from Broadcast TV, Print Media to Research, Brand Consulting to Organizational Strategic Planning, Interactive Media, Digital media to emerging technologies.

Years of erudition inspired Ajay to nurture the canvas of India's social fabric, which in turn made him re-discover himself. Ajay's unique clarity of thoughts enable him to manage his full service Advertising agency with élan and yet his altruistic-at-heart self makes him run a school for specially abled children with equal amounts of sincerity and zeal. And this same passion has made him conceive and create India's first Rural Marketing Magazine "Rural & Marketing" – integrating Urban with Rural markets now as digital portal, www.RuralMarketing.in.

Awarded as ONE of the 50 Most Influential Rural Marketing Professionals of India Ajay has proven his mettle as the Editor-

Awarded as ONE of the 50 Most Influential Rural Marketing Professionals of India Ajay has proven his mettle as the Editor-In-Chief and Technology Expert for print media and corporate communications. Proven ability to fully run an editorial team and grow existing clients as well as winning new businesses.

Recently, ACEF has awarded Ajay, the much coveted Gold Standing, in the Most Admired Rural Marketing Professional Category, in the 9th ACEF Rural Marketing Awards 2020.

Ajay, these days, is investing his time and focus on the latest technological breakthroughs that are taking place in Indian agriculture, and honing his skills in Pro Bono Consulting & Knowledge curation for startups. Today, he enjoys a distinct credit of having transformed many entrepreneurs, business owners and companies into successful leaders, and brands in the country.

Scan to reach my page

www.ajayadlakha.org

Linkedin https://www.linkedin.com/in/ajay-adlakha-20a9a336/

Youtube https://www.youtube.com/user/RuralMarketingIndia

Facebook https://www.facebook.com/ajay.adlakha

Twitter https://twitter.com/ajay_adlakha

Instagram https://www.instagram.com/adlakhaajay/?hl=en

How will this book help

5 Big Promises

1. *Reduce your journey of becoming a valuable & scalable brand by 4 to 10 years*

2. *Save minimum 20% on your marketing expenses*

3. *Develop respect and honour for the next generation*

4. *Templatise your marketing collaterals to reduce your losses*

5. *Know the sequential secret behind any brand*

Leading To: A Purposeful Business that is Globally Scalable

"Dare to be different and see where it takes you."

Acknowledgement

First and foremost, I would like to thank God for providing me with the strength and courage to complete this book. Without Him, I would not have been able to keep my calm throughout the process.

Before I begin, I would love to thank my mentor Akshay Yadav who pushed me to write this book. Another of my amazing mentors is Rajiv Talreja who showered his guidance and patience in helping me to bring this book to life.

I would like to thank the interviewees Anita Nayyar, Bharat Avlani, Harish Bijoor, and Vivek Jain for their valuable interview because their answers helped me in shaping broader perspectives throughout.

I am highly indebted to Sougat Chatterjee and Sunil Khosla for their valuable contribution and also for showing equal passion towards this book as mine.

I would also like to extend my sincerest gratitude to my Infinity Advertising Services team for their dedication and hard work during this entire process. Without them, I could not have completed this book. I am especially thankful for their enthusiasm and support throughout the entire process. From the very beginning, they were always willing to lend a helping hand and provide valuable feedback.

My writers Sandeep Banerjee, Avijeet Sen, Srishti Surana, Bobo Meitei, Ajay Kumar Prasad and Santosh Kumar Jha deserve special recognition for their patience, guidance, and invaluable advice. Their keen eye for detail and constructive criticism helped me to make this book the best it could be.

I am also grateful to my publisher, Dinesh Verma from Pendown publication, and his entire team for taking a chance on me and believing in my project. Without their unwavering support, I would have been unable to bring my vision to life.

I would also like to thank my family, my brothers, Vijay and Tarun Adlakha, my daughters Harshita and Ansuya Adlakha, and my wife, Rajni Adlakha for their unconditional love and support. They have always been there for me, through thick and thin. They have encouraged and inspired me to pursue my dreams and never give up.

I am also grateful to my friends who have supported me throughout this project. They have always been there for me and have provided me with valuable insights, which have helped me to become a better writer.

I would also like to thank the many people who have read my book and provided me with constructive feedback. Their words of encouragement and kind words have been invaluable and have helped me to become a better writer.

Finally, I would like to thank all of the readers who have taken the time to read my book. It has been a long journey, but I am grateful for your support throughout the entire process. Your kind words and feedback have been a source of motivation and have helped me to stay on track.

I thank you all from the bottom of my heart and I hope that you have enjoyed reading my book.

Introduction

Tables turn when passion prevails.

Thums Up, Bisleri Saga:

Back in the late 70s, it was entrepreneur Ramesh Chauhan's foresight and passion that led him to create 'Thums Up' as the most powerful and indestructible brand in the cola market. As a result, Thums Up went on to challenge the might of global cola giants like Pepsi and Coke and simultaneously enjoy double the market share of both the cola makers.

Coca-Cola, the American drinks giant entered the Indian fizz market and amassed enormous profits over a span of 20 years. However, the market didn't really pick up until the Indian Foreign Exchange Act was implemented in 1974 and Coca-Cola had to abandon its operations in the country.

Taking the advantage of this golden opportunity, the Parle brothers, Ramesh Chauhan and Prakash Chauhan launched Thums Up, adding to their portfolio of aerated drinks. Regional competitors like Campa Cola, Dukes, and Double Seven couldn't give Thums Up a tough competition. Ramesh had a vision and he really worked on it.

Under his direction, Thums Up a held a monopoly in the market for nearly 20 years, uniting the youth of India using handsome branding tactics and presenting it as a refreshing cola drink. Later, the brand moved towards masculine and individualistic positioning.

It was only after liberalization that Thums Up encountered a fierce competition from Pepsi and Coke, which caused things to alter. Later, Thums Up, which enjoyed a significant share of the market, was sold to Coca-Cola.

However, the American giant focused its time and energy on developing Coke as the unbeatable brand in the category. It is also believed that Coca-Cola tried to kill Thums Up. Irrespectively, the giant had to bear the brunt of not capitalizing on the brand image that Thums Up had been enjoying for years. People were not comfortable with Coke or Pepsi because by then, the youth had developed the taste of Thums Up and started associating themselves with it. They were not ready to break their connection with the brand. Coca-Cola realised that killing Thums Up would actually mean losing sales.

Thereafter, he created another iconic brand, 'Bisleri,' potable drinking water, and made the consumers hooked to drinking bottled water.

Such was the passion of the entrepreneur that this time he chose to sell the brand to TATA—another trusted and valuable Indian company to keep up the legacy of his brand, despite having multiple offers from Indian and foreign companies.

Ramesh Chauhan is the man behind the success of the soft drink brand. He initially sold soft drinks in tiny bottles in local markets before eventually growing the company to encompass a complete production facility. Chauhan wanted to improve the drinks' flavour and not just sell them. By experimenting with various flavours, he created the distinctive flavour of Thums Up, which is now quite well-liked. To make sure that consumers were aware of the brand, he also made investments in marketing and advertising initiatives. Without Ramesh Chauhan's dedication to Thums Up, the brand image it conveyed would not have been conceivable. His actual implementation on the ground and the brand's goal worked really well together. Ramesh Chauhan created and nurtured the brand that went on to have a high value.

Ramesh Chauhan was able to stand out because he genuinely learned the science and art of creating a brand.

I, hereby, would take a moment to tell you 'Why Nobody Cares For Your Brand.' Let me spill the beans, it's the entrepreneur and his lack of passion for his brand. Ramesh Chauhan's success and that of his brands were fuelled by the proper enthusiasm, which every business owner should have for his organization. There are numerous such entrepreneurs who have been successful in building legacy brands while there are many more entrepreneurs who are struggling to do so.

But, hey, don't sweat. This book will help entrepreneurs to traverse through the various stages of brand building. Let's close the distance between "who you know" to "who knows you."

This book is a quick insightful guide for entrepreneurs here to help them nurture and build a larger-than-life brand. A carefully thought-out branding strategy may do wonders for your brand. It doesn't matter which industry you work in as long as you adhere to the disciplined process of fostering advocacy, scalability, growing awareness, and empathy.

You have the key to winning over devoted customers, starting a revolution, and making a difference. Unlock the treasure to learn a few branding secrets.

Chapter - One
Why nobody bothers

Why Nobody Cares For Your Brand & What To Do About It

Well, let me begin this conversation by asking you "What are you doing to build your company's reputation?"

And why do you think nobody cares about your brand?

The reason is pretty straightforward; people don't care about your brand because it is NOT A BRAND!

A brand isn't born; it is created.

And its creation takes efforts, right processes and techniques. And here I declare that it is the primary duty of all business owners to develop their brands and carve out a distinctive niche for themselves in the marketplace through effective branding techniques. The entire process of branding is scientific and professionals are there to guide one through building brands.

In today's times of crowded marketplaces and the decreasing attention span of consumers [shockingly today, our attention span is even lesser than that of a Goldfish's, which is just 9 seconds], I know it has become increasingly challenging for you to draw the attention of potential customers.

For a moment, visualize that you, me and a few more of your friends are gathered together in a room, and I ask each of you to give me a currency note. Now each of these currency notes will have a certain value, and it is likely that not everybody will give me currency notes of the same value. Someone will come up with a 2000 Rupee note, another with 500 perhaps or 200, 100 or 50 even.

What if I put all these notes together, mix them up, and then randomly hand them out to each one of you? You might not all get the same value note back as you gave.

If the person who gave Rs. 50 gets back a Rs. 2000 note, he/she would be delighted. Whereas a person who gave Rs. 500 and got back Rs. 200 would be unhappy. So what's important here, the NOTE or the VALUE?

It is the VALUE that is important, of course, and so is the case with your business—even more important than your product or service is your BRAND & its VALUE.

Also, tell me something, do you think your Indian currency would be useful if you took it in America or Europe? Think carefully. Would you have to burn up all your Rupee notes if you moved to the US because they were just useless papers?

Of course not; you would simply exchange them for Dollars, right?

The value might not remain the same, but you would still have wealth. Similarly, a brand is a currency that is global. Once you build a brand, the world is your playground; you can take it anywhere.

Like the exchange of currency, you might have to tweak it to suit the local requirements, but it would be valuable anywhere in the world.

In short, branding is the overall interactive experience you create for your consumers, which promotes recognition and motivates them to choose you over and over again. And this branding then translates into exponential sales and profitability.

This is where branding comes in, my friend—It allows you to differentiate yourself, grab attention, build value and occupy space in your potential customers' mind so that in the final moment of reckoning, they choose you.

WHAT IS BRANDING?

So let's talk about what actually is branding. If we were to look at the dictionary meaning of branding, it is highly misleading and limited.

If you look up the Cambridge Dictionary, says, branding is the act of giving a company a particular design or symbol in order to advertise its products and services.

Branding, in effect, is way more than that. It is not limited just to your logo or your visual aesthetics.

For any business to be successful, branding is a must. You need to create a distinct identity for your business/products/services and tell the customer exactly

O   Who you are

O   What you do

O   What solutions you provide

O   What differentiates you

O   Why they should choose you

A well-planned branding strategy can work wonders for your business, irrespective of the industry you are in, provided you follow the disciplined process of building growth, awareness, empathy, scalability, and advocacy in a seamless and cohesive manner.

This will be evident to you from the client case stories that I am sharing with you below and will continue to share throughout.

To begin with, I am sharing with you the fascinating journey of a shoe manufacturer named Dharamvir Singh.

This will give you a picture of how a lot of businesses (especially family-owned ones) are struggling to scale up and are even facing the end of the road because the next generation doesn't want to be associated with them.

So let's deep dive into Dharamvir's fictitious life and business based on true scenarios.

"A brand is a Global Currency that touches all the 5 senses of the consumer."

- Ajay Adlakha

THERE ARE 1,349
CAMERAS IN
THE MARKET.
HOW DO YOU
DECIDE WHICH
ONE TO BUY?

Presenting you a story, based on true scenarios

From Scratch to Stagnation: Dharamvir Singh's Journey

Dharamvir Singh had started small, and he had a shoe manufacturing unit in a nameless street in the town of Agra. He made three pairs of shoes each day, to begin with. It was a craft he had inherited from his father, who had spent his life working as a local cobbler. However, because of the meticulous attention, he paid to each pair and his ability to deliver them on time, demand for his footwear increased.

People in the neighbourhood knew him as a fine shoemaker, and he lived up to their expectations. But then over a period of time, he made the mistake of ignoring his customers by neglecting the quality of his products. This negligence immediately created a reputational crisis for him. However, he realized and owned up to his mistake really quickly. He immediately apologized to the customers, thus restoring his reputation, and continued building the brand.

At that point, he committed to himself that he would work with a sense of morality as well as a social obligation towards his customers as he had a reputation to live up to, and that reputation was why people chose his products.

People perceived him as accountable and well-mannered, and, most importantly, they believed that he made good quality shoes.

His business continued to grow. Within two years, he had to employ someone to assist him. Then in the succeeding years, it became a five-people company. Later, he named and registered his business as Singh Shoes Private Limited.

As his business flourished, the nameless street from where he operated his factory became known as Singh Shoes Street. He figured out a strategy to expand the business and soon addressed the pressing issues. He scaled up production since his target market was expanding. He expanded beyond Agra and later beyond Uttar Pradesh and the northern region.

It took him fifteen years to make Singh Shoes a two-crore company. He enrolled his two sons and daughter in renowned international schools, and he had plans for them to study abroad. After a few years, he decided to go big. So he started contacting major shoe brands in India and managed to secure a manufacturing contract from one of the major brands.

From one, it went up to two, and after some years, it reached three. Thus his reputation as a shoemaker kept growing. That also changed the size of his business which was now about to touch Rs. 20 crore.

This development in his footwear manufacturing business coincided with the liberalization of the Indian economy. Within a few years, he witnessed an entire change of scenario. Many new brands entered the industry; the manufacturing process became more mechanized, and operations began to be supported by skilled workmen.

But he didn't stop there; from a contractual manufacturer for major Indian brands, he went on to secure manufacturing contracts from some of the major global brands.

What followed was something big and personal. He launched his own brand and named it Maza Shoes. Dharamvir launched a collection inspired by some of the brands he had been working with. Using his established network and injecting fresh capital, he made his products available at some of the leading multi-brand outlets.

The opening of a few upscale Maza Shoes stores added to this. He adopted a two-pronged approach, which contributed to the steady growth of his business. This was complemented by the opening of a few exclusive Maza Shoe outlets. For him, it was now a two-pronged business, but his business was nevertheless steadily growing. A major achievement was that he was able to position his brand as a player in the segment he was operating, and consequently, he was able to gradually shift from contract manufacturing to concentrating solely on his brand. This enabled him to gradually transition from contract manufacturing to focusing entirely on his brand.

Fast forward to today, Maza Shoes is a Rs. 200 crore-plus business with twenty exclusive outlets in some tier 2 and 3 cities, and its products are available at several multi-brand outlets. The success that he has garnered over the years has enabled him to invest more in human resources, as given his children an Ivy League education, and he now employs more people. With the huge amount of wealth that he has amassed, he could now afford overseas education for his children also.

His children's expectation was that they would join the family business someday. Although Dharamvir has successfully built a Rs. 200 crore-plus brand and his foreign-educated children have returned, he now realizes that Maza's growth has become virtually stagnant. Or he is not able to take it beyond that. He has tried all means to turn it around, but in vain. They haven't helped.

So, let you and me take a look at some of the major challenges that have hindered the growth of Maza:

1. His children aren't interested in the business. It just doesn't excite or motivate them. They feel that there is nothing interesting for them in the family business; they would rather be a part of a modern workplace.

Had it been Nike or Pepsi, they would have jumped in with great enthusiasm to prove their worth.

They feel that it's merely about stepping into their old man's shoes. There is no real space for them to experiment or introduce new ideas, and any attempt to do so could only entail a clash between the old and the new.

2. Scalability is a major challenge. Since its footprint hasn't expanded and its survival is dependent on stagnant demand, scaling up is a major challenge. Maza's exclusive outlets are doing just fine and the multi-brand outlets are giving him more or less the same sales figures. A large surge in sales is beyond his imagination at the moment.

It can be attributed to a lack of access to the latest technology and a shortage of raw materials, to mention some. Since small businesses lack funds; they cannot afford the latest technology and bulk buying during the season to enjoy the economies of large scale.

3. The brand doesn't inspire respect. Although, Maza Shoes is a recognized name and its market reach has grown. The brand is still not a household name. In other words, it isn't Salvatore Ferragamo or a name that people aspire to own its products or be identified with. At times, people even make fun of the name as it is an affordable brand. Whose children would like to hear their friends say 'the shoe brand that gives immense pleasure' with a tint of mockery about their father's business behind their back?

4. Unable to draw talents to enhance the business. Like most businesses in a similar state, Maza has not been able to bring in talents who could transform the business as well as add more value to the brand. After all, why should talented or efficient people with experience vie to enter a business like Maza? It isn't Apple or Tata. His employees are mostly mediocre kinds who could be mistaken for people stuck or have nowhere else to go.

5. Crisis management has proved to be more challenging. In the age of social media and fast-paced communication, a single tweet by a customer or a news item can either break or make a brand. Such a scenario demands a sophisticated understanding of how communication works in the age of social media and how the same can be used to nurture a brand. Dharamvir has identified the problem, but to ensure that no crisis goes out of proportion, he needs the situation to be handled delicately.

The question that keeps him awake at night is:

WHY NOBODY CARES FOR HIS BRAND?

It troubles him immensely when he drives past a Nike store thronged by customers who are his children's age. It instigates a certain degree of paranoia. However, this doesn't mean that his business has hit the cul de sac.

He has to find ways or introduce certain measures that he should implement rigorously. In layman's terms, he should find the remedies for the maladies.

Being a small or a mid-sized company doesn't mean that it cannot cross the threshold and become a thousand-crore company.

The reality is that Dharamvir isn't alone. There are thousands of Dharamvirs facing the same or similar business challenges.

Of course, they all want to grow and become a thousand-crore business, employing thousands of people with offices scattered across the globe.

But to cross the threshold, the business owner, be it a startup or a family business needs to understand the Science of Branding.

One that seemingly looks simple, and yet not an easy undertaking.

From the above illustration, it must be clear to all of you that all of Dharamvir's challenges exist because he has failed to brand himself correctly.

Lack of Branding can be Fatal

So many family-run businesses are dying a painful death these days because they continue to do business the old way and are focused only on pushing their products or services and fail to see the importance of branding.

They fail to understand that no sales or marketing activities will be fruitful unless they create a distinct brand identity and differentiate themselves and thereafter, then market themselves in alignment with their brand identity.

While they may be spending a lot of money on marketing, their marketing is all haywire, and there is no consistency in the message, the visual representation, the colours, fonts, voice, etc. As a result, it leaves no impact on the customers' minds, and owing to that since there is no impact, there is no retention or recall.

Moreover, the following generation is hesitant to carry on the family legacy since many family enterprises have become dull and stagnant organizations. As a result, years and generations' worth of labour goes to waste, all because of a lack of branding. And since these family businesses have become boring, stagnant entities, the next generation is reluctant to carry on the family legacy, and years and generations' worth of hard work goes down the drain—all due to a lack of branding.

The same is the case with advertising; no matter how huge your advertising budget is, nothing will work unless you sort out your branding first and then advertise and communicate in alignment with your brand identity.

*"Every business that appears
to be breathing its last or having
frequent hiccups should revive itself
through the oxygen of branding."*

Chapter - Two

The book and me

Who am I, and Why Should You Listen to Me?

At this point in our conversation, you are probably wondering who I am and why in this world should you be having this conversation with me, right?

Okay, let's remedy that right away. Allow me to introduce myself.

Hello, my name is Ajay Adlakha, and I am a branding specialist.

My tryst with 'Brandvertising' (Branding + Advertising) began 25 years ago. Ever since, it has never failed me in terms of establishing lasting relationships with multiple clients, multiple brands, and multiple categories of products/services.

I live and breathe 'Brandvertising' every day. It continues to be at the top of my mind and is my most powerful tool to deliver measurable results continuously.

Over many years of working with multiple clients, ranging from entrepreneur-run brands to MNC-led brands, I have developed critical insights and expertise in this area and have worked on almost all the pillars of marketing.

The journey so far has been insightful, brilliant, and rewarding.

And now, my objective is to share my learning and expertise in decoding the science of branding with other entrepreneurs. Trust me. I talk about 'Brandvertising', and I speak from my experience.

WHY THIS BOOK AND WHY NOW?

About This Book

First, let me share with you how this book will benefit you. This book will not only help those in business currently to position themselves as a brand with minimal efforts and costs, but it will also help the next generation. Those who are planning to be a part of the family business legacy and take it to even greater heights of success. They will be able to save millions of dollars by just getting the purpose in place.

If you truly imbibe and apply the science of branding and my specially designed USA framework, I promise you that you will be able to:

- Not only scale your business to the next level, but you will also be able to reduce your journey of becoming a valuable & scalable brand by at least 4-10 years.

- Scale your brand valuation to 5x, 10x, and so on.

- Establish your Brand with at least 20% less spending on your Marketing Budget.

- Ensure Brand respect & Honour in the mind of the next generation's successors.

- Template your marketing collaterals to reduce your losses.

This book will not only help you save money but will also stop the exodus of employees, curb wasteful marketing expenditures, and overcome bottlenecks to achieve scalability by bringing purpose to the organization and the team. Purpose to scale, purpose to innovate, and purpose to understand:

- Who are you?

- What do you do?

- Who needs to know about you?

- Why does it matter?

- How can they find you?

Answering and fleshing out the answers, steps, and actions to all these questions is the first step to exponential and sustainable profitability through the science of branding. This book will show you how to do so smoothly.

Why This Book?

Let me also share with you why I decided to write this book. One, being in love with branding, it breaks my heart to see how people neglect, abuse, or misrepresent brands and lose out on the opportunity to build a profitable empire.

So my sole purpose in writing this book is to guide entrepreneurs and business owners like you on the right track to supersonic profitability.

Two, time and logistical limitations prevent me from personally connecting with everyone who wants my help.

This book is my gift to you, all the business owners and startup owners, to prevent owners from making mistakes that entrepreneurs commonly make by sharing with you my learning experiences and expertise.

If you follow the principles and techniques shared in this book, I assure you that these will steer you to a path of success with the branding exercise.

Chapter - Three

Myths of branding

Okay, so we have been having this conversation about branding for quite some time now. Before we proceed any further, what do you say, should we bust some myths together?

There are so many misconceptions related to branding that prevent businesses from succeeding and keep them trapped in a stagnant plateau of status quo instead of reaching the pinnacle of growth.

And like I said earlier, the entire goal of this book is to help you, as entrepreneurs understand the importance and benefits of branding and help you scale up and become profitable.

So, are you willing to dispel some myths?

Myth 1: Branding = Company Name and Logo

The biggest and most fatal myth exists that every business needs to shatter is this:

Everyone believes that the company name and logo are your brands.

Well, this is only the partial truth; these two things are vital and perhaps the most visible part of your branding but remember they are not the only parts of it. A brand, as we have already discussed in detail in the previous chapters, is a complete identity with many components. The name and the logo are just representations of your brand.

A brand is the entire interactive experience as a whole: It is what customers associate and perceive about your business/ product/service. Branding is a collation of touch points where the customer interacts with you and recalls your business way beyond your company name and logo.

Any business that looks at branding as only a name and a logo is setting itself up for failure.

Myth 2: Branding = Advertising

Another misconception that holds people back and prevents them from effective branding is that advertising and branding are one and the same thing.

Branding is about who you are; it is the core identity of your business, while advertising is the process of communicating and expressing your identity to your customers.

Sure, the two are interconnected but not the same. To be able to advertise well and effectively, you have to brand yourself first.

It will be impossible to create and execute any ad campaign successfully without a clear and focused branding strategy.

Myth 3: Having a Perfect Product/Service is Enough

Most businesses, especially those that are starting out, believe that if they have a great product/service, they do not need to brand, and the product will promote and sell on its own merits.

Of course, yes, a great product/service is critical to the success of any business. However, without proper branding, your product/service won't be able to position and differentiate itself, no matter how great it may be.

It is the branding experience that makes your product/service truly stand out. Branding makes an ordinary product great and a great product even greater.

Myth 4: A powerful Brand Strategy is Built on Features and Not Emotions

In continuation of the above myth, there is another related misconception that branding means talking about the features of the product/service.

That is not true at all! It is one word that drives effective branding: Emotions!

It doesn't matter what it is that you sell or to whom you sell. It could be the most basic of all products/services, or it could be the most complex financial derivative to hit the market ever or the latest cutting-edge technology.

It's not the features that are going to sell it; it's the emotions that will hit homes.

If you want to sell it, the customer has to want it, and they will only want it when they feel it.

You have to brand yourself by telling a story and evoking their emotions.

A brand built around tripping your customer's emotions will always crush competitors who are talking about features and benefits.

Myth 5: The Marketing Department is the only one that's Responsible for Branding

Here's another big myth regarding branding that marketing and advertising departments are the only ones responsible for it.

One great way of putting it is that marketing and advertising departments can be said to be the gatekeepers of how your brand interacts with the public and how it is portrayed to the customers, yet they are not the sole keepers of your brand.

As we have already established earlier, a brand is a wholesome experience in itself that your customer has with your business; therefore, how can it be limited to just two departments? The voice, expression, and identity of your brand are manifested throughout the organization.

Your entire company embodies your brand. Everyone, right from the front office staff, the salespeople, the admin & security staff, the customer service people, the tech support, etc., is your brand ambassador embodying your brand's values, integrity, and identity.

Ensure that your company imbibes the brand values before you communicate them to the customer.

Myth 6: Branding is Expensive and is only for Huge Fancy Businesses

This myth is perhaps the most common misconception that branding is a very costly proposition and only meant for huge fancy businesses with large budgets to spare.

Nothing Could Be Further From The Truth!

Branding is as essential to every organization as breathing is to life. Yes, of course, you need to invest some time and money into building branding collaterals, but it's not just limited to that; it is more about building the overall experience. How do you interact with your target audience, how do your employees respond to the brand, and do they feel a sense of ownership? And how do they radiate this to customers in their interaction with them?

The truth is that all businesses, especially startups and MSMEs, need branding.

Sometimes, establishing and differentiating your brand may be as simple as a matter of improving how you change behaviour internally to make the whole branding experience better for the customer externally.

Difference between marketing & branding

MARKETING	VS	BRANDING
Marketing is how.		Branding is why.
Marketing is short-term.		Branding is long-term.
Marketing is micro.		Branding is macro.
Marketing defines tactics.		Branding defines trajectory.
Marketing generates response.		Branding builds loyalty.
Marketing extracts value.		Branding creates value.
Marketing is the doing.		Branding is the being.

The Most Common Cardinal Sin: Believing that Branding and Marketing are Synonymous

Now that we have been talking about branding and marketing, it's time to bust the biggest myth of all times. It is the topmost common mistake that companies make, and it is the reason that they fail. They believe that branding and marketing are the same.

This couldn't be further from the truth. In reality, they are separate processes and exercises though they are interconnected and do overlap.

BRANDING is all about understanding yourself thoroughly.

As shared earlier in the introductory chapter, it is all about fleshing out the answers to questions such as

- Who are we?

- Whom do we serve?

- What problem do we solve for our customers?

- How are we different?

Thus, branding is the foundation for all further activities.

It is the internal work that you do on your business working from the inside-out.

Before you can communicate to others about what you do, you have to thoroughly and clearly understand what your business is all about.

Before you share your story, you must write, believe in and own your story; only then will you be credible and convincing.

Go deep into introspecting on your business. Here's an example:

Is A Shoe Just A Shoe?

Let's say you make shoes.

Now a shoe is a shoe. Or is it?

There are 1000s of shoe manufacturers in the country all making various shoes in the country.

So what kind of shoes do you make?

Formal, casual or sports shoes?

For men? Women? Or both?

Are your shoes high-end or economy, or in between?

Do you focus on being trendy or being all-time?

Is durability a priority? Or is comfort important?

How are you different?

Maybe you have a famous shoe designer on board who designs your shoes.

Or you use specially imported material for the sole for high cushioning comfort.

Or you give the most value for money.

So are you quirky like Chumbak accessories or posh like Louis Vuitton? These are the identifying questions you need to figure out.

Your story and your values are what sets you apart and impart purpose to your business. It's this story and these values that inspire your own team and build a lasting connection with your customers.

So, understanding your purpose, your why, and the solution that differentiates you, is the core of branding.

Working out what you stand for, what you do, what you provide, who you do this for is the internal aspect of branding, and then there is the manifestation of that purposing through brand names, logos, mascots, color schemes, messaging, etc.

Also branding is a macro exercise, it encompasses your entire organization and the ecosystem.

- It is an identity in the form of a name, just like people have.

- It has a visual identity expressed in terms of logos, stationery, fonts, colors layouts etc.

- It also has a voice in terms of what it says about itself and its relationship with customers, vendors, employees and the environment in general.

- A brand also has its own set of values where it communicates what it stands for, like quality, durability, affordability, etc.

- And it has a personality in terms of the experience it provides its customers.

Thus, a brand is a complete package that defines your business/products/services as a personality.

Branding is an ongoing activity that creates value.

Putting together all this work is called Brand Strategy.

But the bottom line for a brand is to know who you are, what you stand for and what you offer.

The creation and maintenance of brands are becoming more important in today's intensely competitive environment. Investing in branding activities creates brand equity. Equity exists when the customers are aware of the brand, loyal to the brand, and perceive the brand as having quality.

MARKETING is all about understanding your Customer and Communicating with them as per your branding strategy.

"Marketing" is not a straight forward term; it covers a wide variety of disciplines under one umbrella.

It includes areas such as market research, product development, pricing, customer support, websites, brochures, social media, SEO, publicity, public relations, event planning, blogging, community outreach, etc.

Although all these functions and areas can be clubbed under the marketing umbrella, in truth, they all require different skill sets to execute.

> *"Marketing is too important to be left on the marketing department."*

However, simply put, marketing is a process through which your business acquires and retains customers. This process is different not only for different industries but also for different companies.

And to successfully market, it is essential to know your customer.

- The first step is to understand who the target audience is and what it is that they need/want.

- The next step is developing or tweaking products and services that will cater to their needs/wants.

- Then comes the need for positioning those products and services in a way that will appeal to them or resonate with them.

- The final step is communicating and promoting those products and services to the customers so that they know you exist.

Once you are clear on your 'why' and have a branding strategy in place, it is time to take action and get things done. So, marketing is focused and targeted and hence, it is micro.

The trajectory has been defined by branding. The way forward is clear, marketing along with advertising will focus on tactics like campaigns and promotions and these will keep changing from time to time, thus marketing is aimed at short-term goals.

Branding creates value and marketing leverages that value to extract value manifested as business, sales & profits.

So what is a brand

"It is a decision made by your mind and a commitment made by your heart."

The purpose caterpillar is not to live life of a caterpiller but is to Evolve.

Chapter - Four
The journey of an entrepreneur

So, taking this conversation forward let's talk about the journey of an entrepreneur to better understand the timing and criticality of branding. Understanding this journey will truly give you a practical approach towards your brand.

In my years of experience dealing with businesses, typically I have come across three types of businesses. One is, of course, a large business, then there are the medium-sized business, and finally, there are a small business.

In India, for instance, small businesses are typically family-owned. Usually, the journey starts with starting a small manufacturing unit services or retail, which they have either learned or absorbed by working somewhere. That is where they take the idea from and thus start their journey as entrepreneurs.

Since there is something being produced, it is imperative for them to make a sale, which they manage to achieve for some time. Some smart business owners even manage to do a bit of marketing and advertising.

The business owner is happy with the desired results he is getting and the time he is investing. The problem starts when suddenly the business starts going downhill. In such a situation, he has no clue and in panic, he begins experimenting with various marketing tools and is still not able to nail the root cause of the problem.

These are businesses that have not yet decided to get into professional management. The business owner always fears that a professional will ruin the business as he does not trust anyone and feels a third person will not understand the intricacies of the business. The business owner is not qualified to understand and explain the same, so he remains tied to mediocrity.

These are people with very little understanding of markets and marketing, and for them, marketing is a wasteful expense and a sure-shot way to destroy their wealth. So he associates marketing with a negative experience and never comes back to marketing.

However, the key challenge that small businesses need to know is what to focus on. So when I look at small businesses, I keep telling them that the first thing you must forget is advertising, okay?

I keep telling them that you must not be advertising-centric. Instead, you must first be strategy-centric, focusing on formulating your strategy. However, there is this new breed of business entrepreneurs who clearly understands that they need to focus on building their brands too from day one.

Present business owners have started working both on brand and sales & distribution. For them, in the first one or two years, the growth will be a bit slow. However, once the brand starts being visible, then they should think about advertising to fuel its growth.

PUT THE HORSE BEFORE THE CART

So here's my advice to all of you in this situation, always put the horse before the cart. The horse in this case is sales and distribution. And the cart is 'Branding'.

Wherever I've handled small businesses, I have always found this approach working for them. I'll reiterate, never tell a businessman that if he spends three years on advertising, the brand will succeed. Instead, it's crucial to focus on getting the feet of distribution on the ground before organizing your branding strategy. Once your feet are solid and running, as an entrepreneur there are ample options for branding. It is all about creating recognition for your brand in the marketplace. Branding can happen in the marketplace, where the brand will be sold, it can happen in the homes, where people will come out and buy from you.

Today, in the 21st century, managing distribution through E-commerce is gaining traction. Entrepreneurs feel that they need not bother about distribution. The distribution is taken care of by E-Commerce giving them the nationwide reach, they desire.

While in E-Commerce the new brand owners feel this is the best way to penetrate the market but you see this is what I call lazy distribution. They do not have the gumption, or the courage to put their own distribution together and are ready to outsource distribution to somebody. Now, the thing is, it is an easy thing to do.

So, I typically discourage this because when you go to an E-Commerce player, you bleed margins which could be anywhere between 25% and 65%. So, if you really look at it, that is an easy route to take and easy routes don't take you to stardom. Moreover, with E-commerce, your journey of building a brand will end before you would realise.

If you really want to invest, you must invest in something you can own.

Don't invest in something you will never ever own. E-Commerce is something you will never ever own. E-Commerce platforms are interested in their margins, whoever is prepared to pay higher rentals they are showcasing their brands. Moreover, this is automated and supported by an algorithm, it is like getting into the marketplace (*Mandi*) wherein you need to bid on a daily basis and one fine day, if you're not willing to pay that margin you're out. And after that, you can't do anything. So instead of setting up your own feet, you're borrowing other people's feet to run. And borrowed feet can never be yours.

If you invest in your own e-commerce platform, it is yours and won't be borrowed, thus it will yield superior results.

It is extremely important to invest in retail branding, the offline mode. Retail by itself is one of the biggest sciences in the universe; it is a mix of all the sciences—physical, chemical, biological, and all the senses.

As we have discussed earlier, branding is all about emotional connection. Emotions are put into place to understand why people buy and retail branding is really all about getting into the stores and ensuring that the visibility of your brand is terrific. And today, there are a number of ways of creating this. There are professionals providing these services and you're able to amplify this through digital means using the mobile phone through WhatsApp marketing and other digital channels.

And I think one of the killer things, which is not being explored enough by people today is WhatsApp marketing. During the pandemic, you would have seen that the only communication that was alive was WhatsApp communication. Post-pandemic, it has evolved as the strongest communication medium where you can get the message instantly to your consumers.

The business world has understood this and is using this low-cost medium smartly as depicted by the typical journey of an entrepreneur from production to sales and then marketing & advertising **but where the entrepreneur is still failing is in understanding the concept of a brand and a brand valuation that he can get.**

On the other hand, if I ask you to look at large multinational companies with turnovers over 1000 crores you will notice, these are companies that put a lot of efforts into developing their brand.

They fully understand the concept of brand valuation. They have full-fledged team taking care of the brand, strict brand guidelines are followed, and many even go to the extent of auditing this but these are very few. These companies even have full-fledged brand manuals with complete brand architecture.

Teams are regularly trained on these manuals and whenever a new product line is added these manuals are reproduced if necessary and then again they go through the process of training. These companies know very well that any misrepresentation can damage the company and they cannot take this risk.

When any multinational plans to enter any country, they do thorough research before entering, they keep in mind the external factors that will impact them so they study political, Economic, Social, Technological Legal & Environmental factors which are abbreviated as PESTELE analysis. Most important however is the cultural impact so the communication is aligned and looks for partners who can deliver.

However, despite all these efforts, still the brand valuation is not shown on their balance sheet.

Another significant observation I have made in these companies is that sales teams are taking brand decisions. Unfortunately, these teams are only worried about sales and they care a hang about the brand.

This is a terrible situation in large organisations wherein the chariot is pulled by four horses but regrettably in different directions. The brand does manage to grow since they have built a long reputation but imagine how long can a chariot move when all horses pull in opposing directions.

In the context of branding, the four horses are

- ATL (Above the line communication)

- BTL (Below the line communication)

- Public Relations

- Digital communication

Each is held by different agencies and there is no communication between each other, neither they have been trained on brand guidelines and to top this, these decisions are taken by the sales team without any focus.

So, in order to build a brand, you must first ensure that your sales and distribution are on track. Hereafter, branding can prove to be effective for you and your brand.

Brand Stories!

Human beings are wired to emotions, not to reason!

Does this ring true with you? I am sure it does. So, I want you to read this line again and ponder over it in the context of business.

Customers will eventually relate to the emotional benefits even if you boast about the functional ones.

This means that people do not choose your products or services in isolation or because they are the best. They choose to respond to the emotions and experiences that you offer and create around your products/services.

They respond to the story and the storytelling around your products/services.

"Evoking emotions and touching a chord in the customer's heart & mind that compels them to choose you is the essence of branding."

Chapter - Five
Developing your sabotage

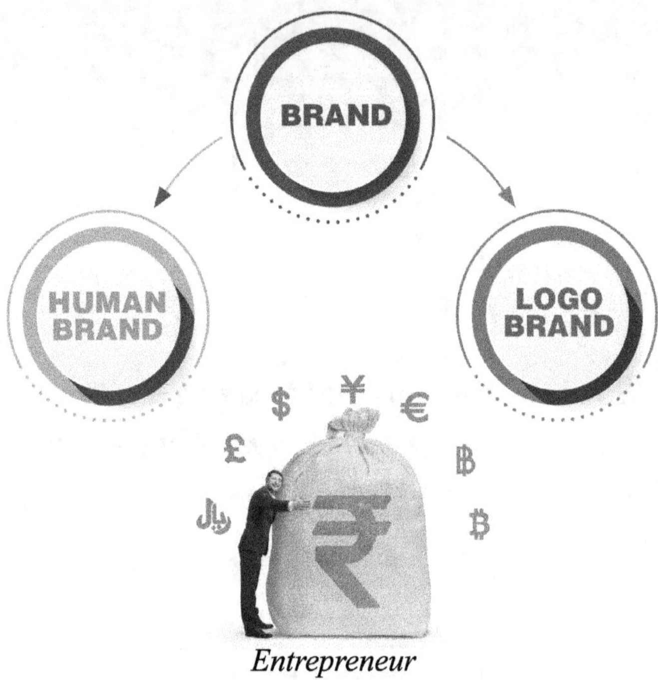

Entrepreneur

Still wondering how to setup your brand?
Let me simplify this for you.
After 25 years of navigating through many brands
and many categories,
I have come to realise that all the brands that exist today
can be segmented into 2 major types:
1. Human Brands 2. Logo Brands
3. Understanding dollar value

1.0

Human brands

It is possible to take your company to the highest levels through personal branding.

A brand is not just an inanimate object or an abstract entity; a human brand is perhaps the most powerful of all brands that exist. A human brand commands respect and privileges.

Look around you, and you can come up with many human brands in their respective fields. Dev Anand, Dilip Kumar, Rajesh Khanna, etc., were all popular human brands in yesteryear Indian cinema. Today Amitabh Bachchan, Ranveer Singh, Deepika Padukone, and Alia Bhatt are the iconic brands.

Sachin Tendulkar, M.S Dhoni & Virat Kohli are the popular human brands in cricket. By virtue of being brands, these people command and attract the best projects, the best directors, songwriters, music directors, co-stars, leagues, etc. They all attract the best endorsements and ads because other brands use these human brands to establish and promote themselves.

Now imagine a business that doesn't need these human brands to promote itself because the business owner is a human brand. In such a scenario, they leverage the trust of their brand to build their company/products/services.

The Face of Patanjali

I am sure you are all well aware of *Baba Ramdev* and his company *Patanjali.*

Almost every day, Patanjali takes out huge ads in newspapers, and their layout remains the same.

Now close your eyes and try to recall these ads; what's the first thing that comes to mind?

Nearly 100% of all the people end up saying Baba Ramdev's picture.

So essentially, Baba Ramdev is Patanjali.

He is trusted as a Yoga & Holistic Wellbeing Guru.

How The Hero Built The Patanjali Empire (Brand)

Most Brands are launched with a product and a company, but not Baba Ramdev; the man is a branding legend in himself. He has succeeded in business by approaching everything atypically and backward. Baba Ramdev launched himself on the Indian centre stage through a free service and not a product or a company. He conducted free yoga camps and talked about naturopathy and swadeshi, completely revolutionizing people's mindsets and lifestyles.

At every camp, he had a captive audience of 10-15,000 people, and he conducted at least 2 such camps in a week, impacting 30,000 people per week. He continued doing this for nearly 10 years and ended up touching approximately a quarter billion people.

These people were ardent followers, deeply connected to his service and philosophy of healing naturally. Usually, a business invests aggressively in customer acquisition and building customer loyalty, but he did it in reverse. He had a loyal customer base ready even before the product came into being.

Additionally, he ignited in people's minds the fire and passion for Swadeshi (products made in India).

Baba Ramdev was by now a widely recognized, admired, and followed personality. In short, he was a BRAND, and he was a HERO!

And voila, then he launched Patanjali, and as expected, people lapped up the product simply because they trusted the Hero- the Human Brand.

However, acquiring customers before the product launch was not the only smart reverse thing he did. He also entered the market in reverse. Instead of targeting the metros, he began the market penetration with the tier 2 & 3 cities. Since he had an exhaustive product mix coupled with his personal credibility as a brand, he convinced local *kirana* (General) stores to become special, dedicated Patanjali Stores, creating a win-win for both.

And throughout this time, he continued to conduct his camps and ignite the fire of Swadeshi in the consumers' minds advancing and promoting Patanjali. In fact, with such a high level of branding, Patanjali achieved what no one had been able to in the past hundred years or so. Patanjali *Chawanprash* managed to topple Dabur *Chawanprash* to the #2 spot claiming the top-rank spot for itself.

Okay, so I want to ask you a question. On the one hand, there are companies like Dabur, Zandu, Baidyanath, etc., who are marketing a product such as Chyawanprash using borrowed credibility through other human brands such as Akshay Kumar, Saurav Ganguly, and Madhuri Dixit or using nameless models posing as regular people.

On the other hand, there is Baba Ramdev, who doesn't need borrowed credibility to sell his Chyawanprash or any other product because he, as a human brand in that realm inspires trust.

Tell me, as a consumer, who would you buy from?

I think the answer is obvious; you will buy the product you trust from the person you trust.

Apart from Baba Ramdev, there are numerous examples of human brands, inspiring huge trust to build big business empires, such as Dr. Naresh Trehan and Medanta, Dr. Devi Shetty and the Narayana Group of Hospitals, Dr. Reddy and the Apollo Group.

Thus, creating and building trust is an essential part of branding

Brand Gandhi

Let me share a few stories to get the perspective right for "human brand heroes." If you were to look at Indian history, the most marketable brand had been Mohandas Gandhi. There are many human beings on this earth who always do things differently. Either they have different personalities or some differentiating traits and/or skills that are visible in the early stages of their life itself. Like Gandhi Ji, while he was in Durban studying and

practicing he had his own newspaper and understood the power of media as a tool, the voice to interact and share his thoughts with others.

Today, if he had commercialized himself, he would have been a brand with the highest valuation in this sub-continent. He was recognized and associated with *Khadi,* the concept of *Khadi,* and the nationwide *Khadi* movement, and in today's scenario, we have the *Khadi Gram Udyog* spread across India, which by itself is a top-notch brand. Similarly, he was recognized for his *Charkha* (spinning wheel) and his *Chashma* (glasses), unique branding logos. Moreover, he is imprinted on Indian currency, which is un-replaceable.

Closer to today's times, taking a leaf out of Gandhi Ji's book is Baba Ramdev (though there is no comparison between the two)

Dr. Devi Shetty: The Hero of the Heart

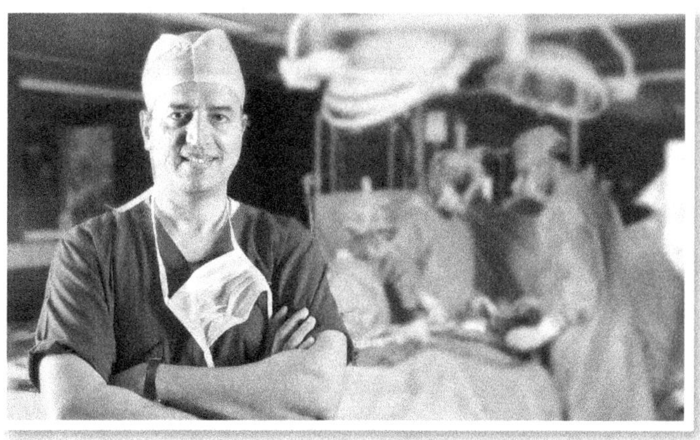

Another amazing "human brand hero" is Dr. Devi Shetty, founder of Narayana Healthcare, a group that is not captive at 1 or 2 venues but is spread across the length and breadth of India with 35 hospitals and 40 collaborative centers.

This hero's first motivation was to make heart care and heart surgery affordable to all. He was determined to bring down the cost from an average of 5 lakh rupees to 50,000 rupees.

To this end, he developed a formula for maximising resource consumption while minimising extra costs.

He pioneered the optimization of OT facilities by lining up 50 beds in the OT so that resources could be utilized to the maximum by a volume of simultaneous surgeries.

He also cut down on any unnecessary frills like air conditioning etc., except where essential, without compromising on hygiene.

All these innovative measures driven by his passion made him a huge human brand. Today the brand, Narayana Healthcare is quite a name to reckon with, and it is all made possible by one person's brilliance and goodwill, the hero brand, Dr. Devi Shetty.

Therefore, one of the key routes you could take to build a business is to build yourself as a HUMAN BRAND and establish your uniqueness to differentiate your product/service/business.

The MDH Grandpa

Another finest epitome of human brands is MDH (Mahashian Di Hatti Pvt. Ltd.), one of India's largest manufacturers and sellers of branded spices. MDH was started by Mahashay Chunni Lal Gulati in 1919 and was officially established in 1959. Today, MDH not just has a pan-India appeal but also exports to various parts of the world, including the UK, Europe, UAE, and Canada. The spice firm may be valued somewhere between Rs. 10,000 cr and Rs. 15,000 cr; in fact, HUL (Hindustan Unilever Ltd.) was in talks to buy a majority stake in the maker of MDH Spices (selling was later denied by the spice maker MDH Ltd.)

Why do you think that a simple spice brand, particularly in a nation where every household would have its own spices prepared at home, became one of the biggest sellers?

Yeah, you guessed it right, 'the famous Grandpa.' The late Mahashay Dharampal Gulati (who died in 2020) leveraged the repetition of his appearance in MDH television commercials brilliantly to establish himself as the brand's face. Success is possible with any brand, simply by adding a personal touch. As the manufacturer himself came out, revealed his personality, and endorsed the products like Degi Mirch, Chat Masala, and Chana Masala, this tactic helped win over the public's trust. The company did not employ any outsiders to promote its spices, and I believe that this tactic helped them get to where they are now and, as a result, became a household name.

Up until the age of 97, The King of Spices continued to sell the goods. That is the authority and trust he had established for both the brand and himself.

The key takeaway from this is that an entrepreneur needs to own his own business for others to accept it. There needs to be a sense of ownership that the 'MDH Dadaji' had for the products. People will only care if you care.

> **A valuable lesson learnt is that you don't need to be a star, or an actor to sell your product. Be a hero to build a legacy.**

At the end of this part of our conversation, my question is:

Are you Branded?

Have you tapped into the emotions of your consumer?

Are you catering to their senses?

Finally, do you inspire trust?

Be yourself. Everthing
Else is Taken!

Eponymous brands: the name game

Elaborating a little further on Human Brands, let's talk about brands that derive their names from the family names or first names of the business owner. What these businesses are doing is leveraging the trust and goodwill earned by the founder or their elders in society.

The positive association with the name makes it smoother to launch products/services, penetrate new markets, and compel consumers to choose you.

These are referred to as Eponymous Brand Names.

Some great examples would be:

Disney Entertainment is named after the legendary Walt Disney.

- Mcdonald's is named after the founders Richard & Maurice family name. Even though Ray Kroc bought it later and expanded worldwide, he still carried forward the eponymous brand name to leverage its value.

- Swarovski is named after founder Daniel Swarovski

- Nutrition & health-related FMCG giant Nestle is named after founder Henri Nestle

- The classic luxury brand Tiffany & Co, an American multinational jewellery & silverware corporation is named after its founder Charles Lewis Tiffany.

Talking about our home turf, there are countless eponymous brands that have built great value and are instantly recognizable.

Some great examples are:

- The Tata Group is named after its founder Jamshedji Tata.

- The Godrej Group is named after its co-founders Ardeshir & Pirojsha Godrej.

- The Mahindra Group is named after two of its three co-founders, JC & KC Mahindra.

- The Bajaj Group is named after its founder Jamnalal Bajaj.

- Dr. Reddy's Laboratories is named after Dr. K Anji Reddy.

Fun Facts: What's In A Name?

The brand Adidas is a mix of its founder's first and last names-*Adi Dassler. Starbucks is* named after a fictional character from the popular book Moby Dick. *Tesla,* the electric car brand was named after scientist Nikola Tesla 50 years after his death.

Naming a new product on an ad hoc basis potentially leads to brand confusion, brand damage, and the loss of an opportunity to build brand platforms to support future strategies. Instead, a new product should have a brand that will support the new offering, will enhance the brand, and will be effective in needed roles when additional products make their appearance. Branding new products strategically involve working with the brand relationship spectrum where descriptors, sub-brands, endorsed brands, and shadow endorsers are employed to control the distance from the master brand. A sub-brand will allow some distance from a master brand, an endorsed brand, a shadow endorser even more, and a new brand the most. (Tell a story behind your name and it will be a memorable part of who you are) the right name captures the imagination and connects with the people you want to reach.

All in the Name

Ran out of necessities right before a party? A friend unexpectedly showed up? Tea craving at 1:00 am? I can guess where the inconvenience must have led you— the 24Seven?

Your one-stop shop in each of the aforementioned cases has been 24Seven, the convenience store. Why? Simply because the brand has always presented itself as available twenty-four hour a day, seven day a week. It has everything you might possibly need, from cigarettes to condoms to prepared food, and of course, chai. The brand, which lives up to its tagline "Awesome through the day, Awesome through the night," constantly adapts and updates to satisfy the needs of urban consumers.

The brand name, which so effectively captures the right essence and demonstrates that it is all for the people, even if they need something in the middle of the night, is what really worked in the company's favour.

The brand rightly identified the problem, and the target audience and then emerged as the solution to them. Brand positioning has been quite effective by simply using a name that implies availability as the solution and became the new age *kirana* store.

Not just the name, but the logo, the modified "location pin" with a quirky owl on it, also clarifies their willingness to serve the consumers, especially during the night, making it the ideal destination or location to shop.

All 24Seven stores throughout have kept their vivacious and upscale ambiance. Because of the striking green and black facade and the welcoming interior design, there is unanimity, making it possible for customers to recognise the store from a great distance. This is quite intelligent. In people's minds, the brand is quite well-positioned. 24Seven has the capability to scale up and become international. The multidimensional approach and the expression of itself have been the major selling point throughout and this could work wonders to gain traction globally.

Hence, a carefully chosen name can sustain a company for all eternity.

Brand concept.. explained

The hero brand concept

An entrepreneur needs to clearly understand the human and hero brand concept. For every organization, three things are critical, a hero (the owner of the company), a company (includes logo, and name), and a product.

For instance, Baba Ramdev is the face, the hero of his burgeoning empire, Patanjali, his company, and ayurvedic products like Chyawanprash, Dant Knati, etc. are the products. Now, your hero must be the face of the company as well as the products you sell. This gives gravity and human touch to your brand, products, and services.

The hero is what drives the organisation and the products, despite the fact that most people work hard to promote their firm and its goods. The business is driven by the entrepreneur's health and brand vision in an entrepreneur-led organisation. Additionally, this concept will give credibility to your brand and eliminate the need for dependency on lending borrowed credibility to your brand by hiring outsiders, like celebrities to endorse your products and company.

As a human hero brand, you reflect your own glory and hence, there is not need to bask in others' reflected glory!

Caution: In the case of the human brand, the reliance on the entrepreneur is particularly strong, which means that he must always be in good health. If something happens to the entrepreneur, the firm will disintegrate, hence there must be a balance between Hero, Company, and Product. In the case of MDH, after Dadaji died, every other rival in the same territory got the opportunity to compete through advertising and finally make an attempt to win the market.

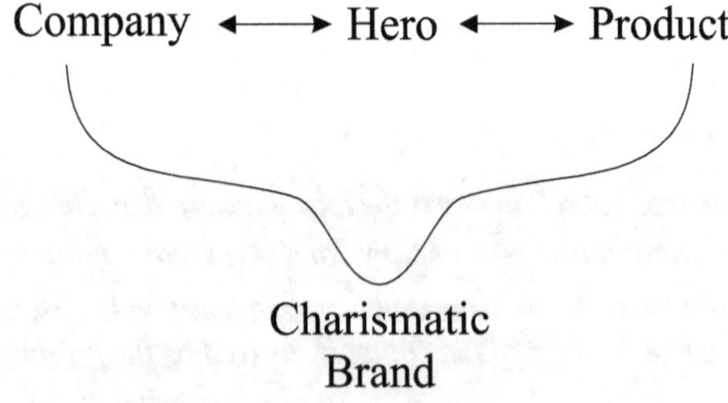

Best investment a brand to do is invest on developing corporate culture.

Good companies don't follow trends, they create trends.

2.0

Logo Brands

An Ageless Beauty With Brains: The Mascot Is The Brand

When we speak of brands and their strong identity, 'Amul-The taste of India' has to make it to the list.

Have you ever wondered why a brand from 1957 still sells like anything? Why is it still trusted to the level that it has become our inevitable choice?

Well, the Amul girl Ms. Utterly Butterly is the answer to all that.

The Amul Girl has been entertaining its audience for the last 55 years but doesn't look a day over 9-year-old.

DaCunha communications, an ad agency in Mumbai is to be credited for this widely loved creation. Whether it is politics, sports, society, entertainment, weather, or infrastructure, the girl has dealt with them all since her inception.

She very well adapted the tone of commenting on current affairs and portrayed them with all her wit and humour. Look, Amul today owns a pronoun - "her" hence, the brand is personified. Over the years, Amul has maintained the girl's distinguishing features, including her blue hair, chubby cheeks, wide eyes, no nose, and long eyelashes.

People still connect with the girl because she has shown her existence constantly in the market. She continues to succeed in building long-term relations with her audience and consumers. The mascot has been the spokesperson for the brand.

So, is Amul anything without the girl?

Most would answer; probably not!

But a word of warning here, let's not confuse mascots with logos.

While mascots may seem like logos, they go a little beyond.

Mascots also act as the spokesperson for a particular brand, sometimes becoming the brand's ambassador. Using mascots can help brands take a back seat when it comes to spending hugely on celebrities.

Also, mascots can be temporary whereas a logo is permanent. There have been times when mascots were dropped off and didn't continue with the brand.

For instance, unlike the Amul Girl, Gattu, the renowned lad for Asian Paints, and Maharaja of Air India had a shelf life of a few decades and were abandoned midway by the brands as

they did not keep up with the changing times. Whereas, the Amul girl continued to evolve and stay relevant.

However, the logo remains constant throughout (with some changes over time). Successful/famous logos will typically have the right mix of colours, fonts, and mnemonics to become smashable and almost instantly recognizable, and then comes the duty and responsibility of every brand to safeguard it.

A logo is so important because it grabs attention, makes a strong first impression, is the foundation of your brand identity, is memorable, separates you from the competition, fosters brand loyalty, and is expected by your audience.

The Power of A Brand Crowdfunds A Movie

Manthan, a movie made in the 70s highlighted the entrepreneurial journey of Dr. Verghese Kurien, the father of the white revolution, in India. It is the story of how the cooperative dairy model founded in Anand, Gujarat with perfect coordination between the company and farmers led to an exponential rise in milk production in the country.

Within a decade, Amul became Asia's largest dairy unit with a production capacity of 20,000 liters per day.

Helmed by director Shyam Benegal, Manthan, with the remarkable song "Mero Gaam Katha Parey," featuring the best of artists in all areas of filmmaking. It won the 1977 National Film Award for Best Feature and Best Screenplay in Hindi.

However, the most interesting fact about the movie was that it was the first time a movie was crowdfunded. And this crowdfunding was made possible only and only due to the power of the brand.

Manthan was produced by the Gujarat Co-operative Milk Marketing Federation Limited. Incredibly, the film was produced with the help of 5 lakh farmers, who contributed Rs. 2 each to make it because they believed in the power of the brand and wanted to contribute to tell its story.

Made with a budget of 10 Lakhs, where each farmer contributed Rs. 2 to make the film, which went on to do exceedingly well, further cementing the power of the brand.

As entrepreneurs, you put all your effort into your services and goods because you know that they are what make you genuine heroes. But in the process, you frequently overlook the logo, which is one of the key elements in forging a brand's identity. Making a logo might not be your top priority, and in the back of your mind, it might even be the last thing you would want to focus on. However, there are countless examples of logo brands with an immense brand value that are absolutely imprinted on the consumers' minds.

Some shining global examples would be Coca-Cola, Apple, Nike, Chanel, Tesla, Shell, Mcdonald's, Starbucks, and Amazon to name a few.

Looking at brands that are more familiar to us, such as Amul, Tata, State Bank of India, Star Plus, HDFC Bank, Airtel, Axis Bank, Bajaj, Doordarshan, Hindustan Petroleum, etc., reveals that they all have a strong recall value and can be easily recognized by their logos.

To better illustrate this, let me use a recent instance of a logo-related conflict between the two Shiv Sena warring groups. Why do you think the Shiv Sena factions fought tooth and nail for the "bow and arrow" symbol? The answer is simple: logo is fundamental and valuable to an organization. Hence, both factions wanted the iconic symbol because it had established a deep connection with the voters and followers.

Having a logo is as important to building a successful business as having high-quality items. Let's look at some examples of how brands have done exceptionally well with their logos in terms of generating revenue, connecting with customers, and intriguing curiosity for other brands so much to show interest in their equity.

The science behind the logo has been kept effortless and easily comprehensible and so it worked for the brand. That is the power of a logo brand.

Logo Power: Local Being Courted by Global

Haldiram's, which was established by Shri Gangabisanji Agarwal in 1937, is one of the best Indian food brands and makes for a wonderful example when it comes to logo branding.

Have you wondered how a tiny shop in Rajasthan's small town of Bikaner now has a chain of restaurants all over the world?

The story begins with the founder Shri Ganga Agrawal who was addressed as Haldiram Ji by his customers and went on to become a household name.

The logo today looks like an intricate design, keeping intact the authenticity that Haldiram's is long trusted with. Haldiram's is written in white letters stamped on a red oval in the Brand's logo, which makes it visible, readable, and at the same time catches attention because of the choice of colours used. Not just this, the logo has been further adorned using a monogram, a motif of the sinuous letters "H" and "R," perfectly interwoven together.

Today, the logo not only represents the brand symbolically but also embodies the trust and authenticity that customers look for. Additionally, Haldiram's sweets and baskets of packaged goods are now being used for gifting during special occasions because the brand has, over the years, gotten associated with class and superior quality.

The Logo Brand has become so popular that it has been repeatedly courted by American giants PepsiCo and Kellogg's to buy a stake in Haldiram's though the family has refused it.

This is the magic a logo (that reflects gravity in the brand) can create.

Make Them Aspire for the Logo & Carry it With Pride

Coach, the luxury leather accessories brand based in New York is a classic example of how a logo can be symbolic of luxury and sophistication.

"A man on a carriage with two horses" is quite a representation of the high-level products of the company. The Coach logo from 1941 remains the same with some slight changes and redesigning in the typeface. The horse-cart logo has been made smaller and COACH, a bit bold.

The brand also uses a boxed octagonal design with curved edges. Today, the brand becomes easily recognizable.

Also, if you have looked at its basic bags, you would find two letters Cs facing each other all over the product. This is how it gets attention from the people around by creating an abundance of the logo and still remaining dignified.

The social status the brand has acquired over the years is strongly correlated with its logo. Coach additionally made sure that the logo was turned into a check, in order to confirm that the bag is authentic.

Therefore, the coach logo within the bag communicates that the company owns it proudly and wants the customer to wear and carry it with the highest pride as well.

Powerful Fun Fact

The power and value of a Logo Brand are undeniably huge. Now see, if you intend to buy a McDonald's franchise, it would cost you near about Rs. 30 Lakhs and 4.0 percent of monthly sales. Being a McDonald's franchisee is no mean task, a huge investment is needed to earn the Golden Arches. The simple grill restaurant has turned into a massive brand with logos being sold in lakhs.

Does a brand have a dollar value?

Brands now appear regularly on balance sheets in many companies. The intangible value of the brand is often much greater than the corporation's tangible assets.

The importance of brand strategy and the cost of building brand identity should be understood at the highest levels of an organization and across functional areas—not just sales and marketing, but in legal, finance, operations, and human resources as well.

3.0
The dollar value of a brand

"*Think brand as assets with strategic value*"

I am sure you are still reeling a bit from the amazing tales of brand power & brand value shared in the previous chapter.

But also, you must have realized by now the importance of brands and brand management. It plays a decisive role in differentiating yourself from the competition, and also in generating profit and shareholder value.

Consumers choose between products via brands. Since a brand name enhances the value of a product and is difficult for competitors to copy, a brand name plays a critical role in marketplace competition.

A strong brand means additional cash flows, because of price premiums and lower advertising expenditures. Besides, its values provide the brand owner with more leverage over retailers and facilitate negotiations with them. As for the retailers, a powerful brand benefits them because their better acceptance reduces the risk of selling.

You might find this hard to believe but a strong brand has a longer life cycle than its products even. And the great thing is this: once you've created a valuable brand, its value and positive image can be transferred to other products or product categories.

This transfer of brand value is more viable than the introduction of a new brand since the chances of a new brand failing are high. Most times, launching new products with a transferred brand in a market is faster and more cost-effective.

When it comes to securing loans from a bank, a strong brand can serve as securities for credits. Normally, firms with valuable brands have fewer difficulties in finding creditors even when they do not have many tangible assets. Besides, they can even weather any storm in times of crises based on the basis of their brand value.

Overall, strong brands are valuable and an important intangible asset to a company.

However, there is a pitfall to watch out for - don't become complacent and don't take your brand and its value for granted; a brand can lose its value. It needs to be managed and controlled correctly. Therefore, effective performance measures and control of the brand is vital in order to manage and control the brand.

That brings us to the most important question that I have been raising right from the beginning.

Does an entrepreneur understand the concept of brand value?

To be honest, the answer is ambiguous. The answer in my opinion is yes and no. Somewhere in the back of their mind, they know that it exists. They also very well know that a brand can increase their cash flows and generate profits over a longer term. But unfortunately they never have time to create one as they are busy firefighting with other things.

Brands today are not restricted to marketing or profits made by a company.

A brand is an expression of identity complete in itself. Brands serve as powerful markers to help consumers express values, display status and generate social personality.

Consumers use their interaction with brands to identify with others and gain admission to a community that may be aspirational.

Seen from a business lens, branding is an integrated strategic approach and not merely a select set of activities. It is the key to creating and maintaining competitive advantage.

A brand's strategy must address key components of value creation such as reputation value, relationship value, experiential value and above all symbolic or cultural value.

It is a part of our everyday life. The term brand refers to names, terms, signs, symbols and logos that identify goods, services and companies; the economic merit of a brand lies in its reputation and esteem. The sociological basis for a brand's valuation is as a trust mechanism. In popular culture, a brand is a story and a symbol. All these markers add to a brand's inherent value.

Brand value is more than just a monetary value, despite the skyrocketing brand valuations.

"Brand value is the 'perceived value,' and how often people will choose one brand over the alternatives. Brand value is important because when people perceive that a brand is distinct and aligns with their personal values, it's a really powerful competitive advantage."

Brand Valuation Benefits

Valuing a brand has the distinct advantage of converting a brand from being an expense on the P & L statement to an asset on the balance sheet.

Companies are spending millions of dollars to create awareness of their products and market their brand. What the company reaps from this expenditure can make or break it.

Your brand is more than the products or services that you sell. It is what you stand for. Your company logo, products, website, or marketing campaigns may and will change with time, but your brand value must never fluctuate, it must always remain the same.

Consumers are looking at connections with brands hence, it is important for companies to relate to and focus on understanding consumers to build a powerful brand.

What Makes A Brand Valuable?

Valuable brands have a few things in common. A brand is considered valuable if it's:

- ❑ Recognized - (people know who they are)
- ❑ Positive Perception - (people have a good view of them)
- ❑ Popular - (people actually buy and use the products or services)
- ❑ Loyal - (customers are ambassadors of the brand)

Some recent examples of brands leveraging their value to make great deals are: Ruchi Soya bought by Patanjali, Hamleys by Reliance, and the recent acquisition of Indian Airlines by the Tata Group.

India's Most Valuable Brands

There are numerous stories of the power of brand value from the world over. The challenge is understanding the concept of brand valuation and how it will help your company to reach the next level, how it will help your external and internal environment to respect you .

It's all about understanding how you can build a legacy by creating a brand like India's MVBs as listed below!

So why then is the money spent on marketing treated as an expense mostly while it should be treated as an investment since it generates brand value that actually translates into Dollars?

- The Tata Group — $19.6 billion
- The Life Insurance Corporation — $7.3 billion
- Infosys—6.5 billion
- The State Bank of India—5.97 billion
- The Mahindra Group—5.3 billion
- HDFC Bank—4.8 billion
- Bharti Airtel—4.8 billion
- HCL Technologies—4.6 billion
- Reliance Industries—4.6 billion
- Wipro—4 billion

The answer is simple. This happens because we don't have any metric measures in place to justify ROI and convince investors and boards.

Brand Strength Index

In this particular area, let me share with you the essence of what Sameer Dixit has said about the Brand Strength Index (BSI).

Therefore, it is necessary to have in place measures that can showcase the brand strength. While organizations spend colossal amounts on studying and tracking consumer behaviour, competitions, demographics, etc,. they make little effort to gauge or understand the brand strength.

Now, the brand strength does not necessarily refer to scores derived from tracking the brand equity or measuring standards of loyalty and intent and the Net Promoter Score (NPS). These measures are very important indeed, even critical, you could say, but they are not enough to base business and investment decisions on.

Ideally brand value/strength should be measured on the basis of an index that is composite and correlates all the inputs (marketing, sales, distribution, products, pricing, footprint, etc) of a corporate with the brand equity that those inputs would generate and then correlating the brand equity to the financial success of the business. This would justify the ROI for the business as a whole.

Today, it is indeed possible to measure every marketing, business, or brand activity to calculate the before and after impact of the activity (yes before it's done too) whether or not it will contribute to the business returns and the strength of the brand, by how much, and across which aspect (competitive or basic hygiene factors).

Why should this be important?

As a rule, CFO's, investors and boards tend to look at ROI from an economic standpoint only and they seek justifications for their investment accordingly. They do not think that marketing perspectives and impacts should also have a bearing on their decision.

They need to understand that a stronger brand drives better financial returns and higher profitability for the business.

A brand is the primary reason why people pay a couple of hundred dollars more for apple products Vs. some of their competitors.

The brand strength index (BSI) therefore is the most critical tool for every company (big or small) to measure the outcome of their activities (internal or external), marketing campaigns or sponsorship, CSR or PR efforts.

It's the only composite measure that can be applied through an organisation with a consistent framework overcoming the challenges of multiple measurements given the diverse business verticals and activities across organisations.

Having a Brand Strength Index (BSI) also helps measure the downside of not doing something or the upside of doing it Vs. some of your own activities as well as competitive activities.

It provides insights about if or not an activity actually contributes to the competitiveness and brand strength in the desired areas or just a wasted effort to keep you visible and afloat.

A Brand Strength Index therefore is a must have decision making, measuring, monitoring and maximizing tool for your business and marketing needs.

The real brand value

So here's an analogy that you all will be able to relate to. When a child is born or even before when parents learn that they are expecting a baby, they start thinking about the name. Parents, grandparents, relatives, and friends all get together to suggest a name.

It is a big decision to be taken indeed.

Then you ask *pundits* for their input on auspicious letters with which the name should begin. Once the letter is finalized, then begins the arduous marathon of deciding the name. You google the best names segregating them into multiple categories—names derived from gods, goddesses and religion, traditional names, and modern names. There are multiple lists to narrow down from, and this mind-boggling exercise continues for a good six to seven months usually.

In this entire exercise, what we are looking at is that the name has to be unique.

Imagine working on a similar principle with respect to building your company or a brand. Your name needs to be unique. However, generally, you don't work that way. You start your brand/business by any name that comes to you (case in point being Maza Shoes and Dharamvir, the case study in Section 1 that we talked about).

Later, it gets challenging when you see that what you are producing is manufactured by millions of people around you, and a unique name or identity would have been a great asset in differentiating yourself.

Typically, the story of any business person runs on a similar line. Either they have worked somewhere and gained experience and access to important data, or they copy tricks of business learned by observation of where they work or their relatives and friends and start their business with minor capital.

The journey is smooth till a certain point, but with time and movement, they wish to scale up, and that is the time they realize that they need to differentiate themselves to survive and thrive in the market.

This smart, unique naming and differentiation of the product by a unique targeting strategy will become outstandingly clear to you through the fantastic branding story of Dabur's Real Juice brand.

The REAL Deal Indeed!

Dabur was the pioneer of introducing packed juices in India in the mid 90s. It was an unheard concept until then.

Now, Dabur played smart on 2 counts.

One was a unique naming strategy. They named the brand, 'Real', which in itself communicated purity and originality, implying health and well-being.

The second unique thing they did was targetting mothers in all their advertising campaigns, even though the real target group was children and adolescents.

Despite its strong distribution network, Real as a product did not generate a profitable ROI. However, through its unique name and branding, it imprinted itself in the minds of mothers as a healthy nutritive option for their children.

This built such a strong brand equity that when Real was valued at about 35-40 Cr, Tropicana (from the Coke banner) entered the juice market. Despite being backed by Coke's phenomenal distribution network and children actually liking the product, Tropicana failed to penetrate the market.

WHY, you might wonder?

The reason was simple. The mothers did not approve of Tropicana; they perceived it as nothing more than a variation of an aerated drink and Real as the real deal—real healthy fruit juice.

The Tropicana Vs Real brand battle continued for 5-6 years while Dabur grew to 100 Cr, pumping a lot of money into the brand with aggressive campaigns and powerful brand ambassadors. Tropicana, with all its might, failed and found it difficult to battle Real.

Finally, they came up with a solution to buy out Real.

Now, this is an the amazing part:

- Real was a 100 Cr company.

- It was not profitable.

- Tropicana didn't want Real's formulation.

- It also did not want Real's factories.

And yet it offered 1,500 Cr as its buyout offer. SHOCKING & UNBELIEVABLE, right?

Actually, not, because that is the POWER of UNIQUE BRANDING!

All that Tropicana wanted was the BRAND NAME: Real!

Your Brand Is Your True Worth

Okay friends, take a thorough look at the pictures.

Can you say for certain that the coffee in these cups is actually different in taste?

And also tell me, if I filled the exact same coffee in all these cups, would you still not be willing to pay differently on the basis of the logo on these cups?

Of course, you would pay based on the logo and how you perceive it.

So, what are you really paying for?

Are you paying for the coffee or the logo?

YOU ARE PAYING FOR THE BRAND VALUE, OF COURSE!

In the previous chapter, I shared with you how Dabur Real, a 100 Cr company, had a brand value of 1500 Cr despite not being profitable.

Similarly, let me share with you the interesting case of 'the battle of inverters.'

The Battle of Inverters: Luminous Leverages Branding to Light up

Be honest; what is the first thing that comes to your mind when I talk about inverters?

At least 90% of you are likely to say Luminous. Yes, that's right, Luminous is considered almost synonymous with inverters.

Interestingly enough, believe it or not, Luminous was not the pioneer of the inverter market. Microtek was the pioneer; they started out in the early 80s, while Luminous came in the late 80s.

Microtek chose to expand in the market through the price route, selling its inverters @ 15 K a piece and focusing on distribution by influencing electric shops and electricians.

While Luminous focused on making the product user-friendly and attractive, however, the foremost thing they did differently was penetrating the market through their promotional and advertising activities, including celebrity endorsements and TV commercials

Today, if you look at these two brands when compared in 2020, Luminous was valued significantly higher as a brand despite Microtek also having a significant market share.

So, take a look at the behind-the-scenes story of Luminous.

When SAR (Sati, Anil and Rakesh) Silicon Systems Pvt. Ltd. launched Luminous, its focus was on inverters to back up household electronics. The product wasn't unique. Any company could assemble or manufacture it. Even someone with the knowledge and access to the parts could assemble an inverter in their garage. Moreover, selling the product was also something just about anyone could do.

But the challenge was building a brand that could be trusted so much that the customer didn't need to think twice while making the purchase.

So, How did Luminous pull it off?

Brand Value as Collateral

When the brand was launched, the target was to alter the way the consumer viewed the product. They wanted to make it a necessary evil. So they injected a certain degree of emotion into the mix to make the brand more aspirational.

SAR advertised the brand on television; the first to do so in that product category in India. It spent 8–10% of the revenue on advertisements on radio and television, especially during cricket matches and Bollywood entertainment shows with high viewership.

After capturing the customers' minds, it moved closer to customers by building and strengthening distribution networks. Then if focused on building trust through services. It installed and serviced all its products on its own.

By 1997, it launched a 24/7 customer care desk and used customer relationship management CRM software to build customer loyalty so that the dealers were also tied, thus they were pulled toward the SAR family.

It turned out SAR's inverter was a superior product backed by strong customer service that replaced or repaired defective products.

However, the disadvantage was that it didn't manufacture the batteries; they were outsourced and at least 8-10% of the batteries were turning out to be defective.

Now the trouble started as the brand owners felt that the battery supplier was pinching the quality and supply. They took the matter seriously as the battery was an important component of the inverter system and withdrew faulty products and refunded customers. This move was a serious part of the brand building exercise.

In 2004, they started looking for a permanent solution to the battery problem. It could mean owning a manufacturing unit or changing the supplier. What was clear was that the brand owner wouldn't compromise on the quality.

The company could have imported the batteries, but that would result in making the product more expensive. After extensive search, SAR found a battery manufacturer in Cyprus it wanted to buy. But raising the capital was the biggest challenge as they had no collateral assets, except the prestigious Luminous brand.

At that time the company had only $2 million on its balance sheet and it needed $11 million to get started as a battery manufacturer.

The owner did the unusual and unheard of in such a scenario: he pledged the brand as collateral.

The bank did the unusual by accepting it, but with the condition that if the loan was not paid back, then it would have the right to take over what was arguably SAR's most valuable asset.

By then Luminous was a well known name and it was a brand known for quality and customer care. The bank understood the underlying problem and placed faith in the brand.

It was the first time in the bank's history to accept a brand name as collateral and extend a loan of $9 million.

THAT IS THE IMMENSE POWER OF BRAND VALUE

However, picture abhi baaki hai mere dost…. The story of the power of brand value doesn't end here, there's more to the story.

The company's desire for new markets and more cash flow to support its bank loans expanded the pressure to create. It set out to raise private equity, and SAR was changed to Luminous TeleinfraTele Infra. In 2007, CLSA Capital Partners and others invested $21 million in the company. This enabled it to diversify its product portfolio. During the global financial crisis in 2008, the company not only survived but also expanded. Overall, annual revenue of the company rose manifold from 2003-2013, reaching $336 million.

With the exponential growth and strong industry forecasts, the company had many options. Several private equity firms were interested in investing in their growth, many potential buyers were courting them and the company was considering an IPO.

In 2011, they settled on a good offer made by Schneider Electric. Schneider considered it because it saw the potential to reach the vast Indian market through the Luminous brand.

74% of Luminous' stake was sold to Schneider for $307 million.

It was reported that the transaction was valued at 16 times the company's 2010-2011 earnings.

Brand value isn't restricted by time. Such is the power of brand value that even time cannot put a dampener on it.

Take the case of Campa Cola, an Indian brand owned by the Pure

Drinks Group, that was a market leader in the soft drinks market during the 70s & 80s but fizzled out due to the re-entry of the international giants, Pepsi & Coca-Cola.

By 2009, Campa Cola was literally dead and had continued to be a walking ghost with barely a presence in the market since then. As a business, it was of negligible value.

Yet Reliance Retail acquired the brand Campa Cola for Rs. 22 cr. recently (undoubtedly a peanut sum for Reliance), way overvalued for the Campa Cola business.

So what did Reliance pay up for?

Yes! You guessed it right: BRAND VALUE

Because even today, Campa Cola has a nostalgic brand value imprinted deep in the psyche of consumers. And that brand value is exactly what Reliance wants.

Taking forward our conversation on the soft-drinks market, let's talk about one of the most iconic brands: Coke or Coca-Cola.

Probably nothing explains the power & value of a brand more than this iconic brand.

As per Statista 2021, Coke's revenue was 33.01 Billion USD$ in 2020. Its annual gross profit was 19 Billion USD $ as per macrotrends.net 2021.

However, can you even take a guess, what the value of the brand Coke is?

I'm willing to wager that the majority of you won't be able to guess anywhere close to the actual figure.

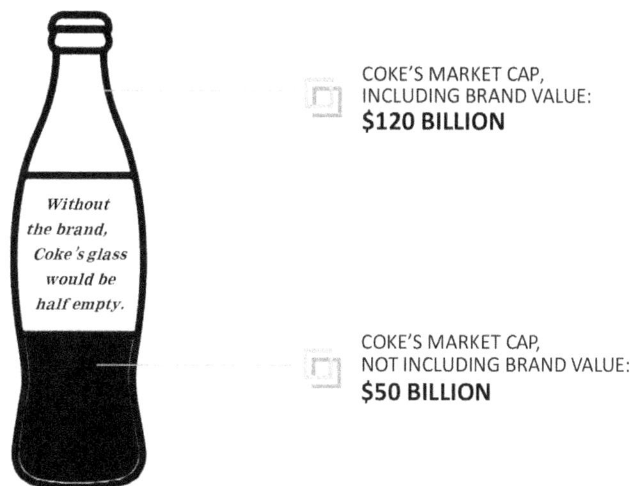

Okay, let me not keep you in suspense any longer…

BRAND COCA-COLA IS VALUED AT A WHOPPING 87.6 BILLION DOLLAR USD$

Now, that is the value of a brand!

Thus, building your brand isn't an option or a choice, it is a necessity. It is the only way to go, because your brand is your true value.

A Fun Fact for You!

I'll use an amusing scenario to demonstrate why brand value is more significant than physical infrastructure: What do you think would happen, for example, if Amul lost all of its production-related assets in a catastrophe? Although, it would be a terrible loss, it is likely that the business would continue to exist and gradually recover.

By contrast, however, if all of a sudden all Amul's consumers fell prey to a sudden short lapse of memory and forgot everything related to Amul, then what do you think would happen? I guarantee you, the company would go out of business in a jiffy.

NOW THAT IS THE POWER OF BRAND VALUE!

Unfortunately, the irony is that in India, the core concept of brand valuation does not exist in the business owner's dictionary at all.

I've given you a tonne of examples of companies making enormous profits because they established and understood brand value.

However, here in India so many people do not understand how to unlock the hidden treasure in the business or brand they have built up.

Meet Sharma Jee, Your Friendly Neighborhood Businessman

Okay, now let me introduce you to Sharma jee, a businessman like many others you would have come across. He is running a successful clinic and at some point decides to retire from the business and wishes to look at some newer opportunities and puts his business on sale.

Most times Sharma jee & other businessmen like him do not even realize that in addition to their business, **they hold the key to another treasure—their brand** (provided of course they have one, either by default or by design), either he could sell his clinic or his brand and both would be treated differently.

After all, he started from scratch and has reached a business of say Rs.100 cr. In the process, **he has created value in the business, but he doesn't know how to unlock it.**

Sharma Jee makes the mistake of only looking at the daily net profit, and investing their money in real estate and the other traditional ways and not looking at exiting the business and unlocking the value base they have created in his brand.

So, this is something which prompted me to write this book, so I could help entrepreneurs understand the value and valuation of creating and owning a brand.

Now, when Sharma Jee understands the value of creating or having already created a brand, he will face one of the two paths in life, either his next generation will respect his brand value and join the business to take it forward, or he will have a brand value that he can leverage to negotiate a profitable sale for his business as well as the brand value instead of having to sell the entire business either at discount or at par making him happy that he has saved his accumulated real estate and his business is also sold .

Right now most entrepreneurs end up selling businesses not brands.

However, I am confident that after reading this book, the scenario will change completely.

A ray of light is already visible. There are these emerging companies like Zomato, Cred, Urbanclap, Grofers, img, etc, these new age businesses when go into business understand the value of a brand and are all out to build valuation.

Though these are in their nascent stage, they very well understand that it is not just the product, sales or distribution, there is something bigger they need to unlock and while creating their brand they have clearly understood the power of technology that will enable them to build valuation. These companies are examples that what was usually being achieved in decades can be achieved in merely a few years with the science of branding.

So, through all these stories, I hope you are grasping the significance of brand value.

Brand value isn't merely about an entity's revenue generation capability. It is, in fact, the brand's perceived value in the customers' eyes and mind.

Use the science of branding to ensure that every branding activity you indulge in is customer-centric.

Because your brand value is always way more than what your business is valued at, anywhere from 10 X to even 100 X.

Chapter-Six

The game of branding

Charismatic Branding

A Charismatic brand is any product, service or organization for which people believe there is no substitute.

A charismatic brand is one that has a perfect balance in catering to the functional and emotional needs of the consumers. There are many brands whose major focus is on creating emotions while they subtly give functional benefits.

Growing significance of emotional needs in the consumption environment is something you as an entrepreneur really need to understand and work on.

In the earlier chapters we have looked at many stories of companies capitalizing on emotions and emotional connect to build their brand.

Emotions are a composite of experiences consisting of behavioral responses, significant results, physiological reactions, and subjective feelings.

Marketers understand without a doubt that branding is crucial–branding is what enables your brand to stand out and differentiate itself amongst a vast sea of competitors.

A successful brand is so much more than just its logo, its success stems from its emotional connection with its customers as we saw in the case of Amul, Real and Patanjali earlier in the book.

Emotional branding clearly differentiates companies from their competitors.

It helps to create deep long-lasting bonds between the brand and its consumers. Such emotion based relationships are not easily destabilized by the temptation of other brands as compared to relationships based on price or convenience.

Only an insight-based, personalized marketing approach can form a strong enough bond with a brand that evokes a personal, emotional reaction in customers. And brand marketing through social networks makes it all the more important that brands strive to build connections with their customers on a personal level.

Creating an emotional bond with customers requires more than good marketing – a company engaged in emotional branding puts the needs of its customers ahead of the product selling.

Key brand stakeholders

Remember, at the beginning of our journey, we came up with the conclusion that if you are not branding right, no one cares for your brand.

So now that brings us to a logical question, who are these people who should care about your brand? .

These are your brand stakeholders.

Okay! Okay! I know the next logical question: Who or what are brand stakeholders?

Simply put, brand stakeholders are people who have an interest in how your company performs.

Don't ever make the mistake of thinking that your investors and your customers are your only stakeholders.

Studying the diagram above will give you a clear picture of how extensive your brand stakeholders are.

Your positioning, reputation and goodwill extend much beyond your target customers. There is a large group of people who impact and are impacted by your brand.

Even employees are key stakeholders in your brand. Employees are now known as 'Internal Customers' since their power is far-reaching.

Gaining insight into stakeholder characteristics, behaviour, needs, and perceptions, catering to them accordingly will help your brand succeed and yield high returns.

Overlooking even one stakeholder could mean overlooking a business opportunity and result in loss.

However, a word of caution here. The various stakeholders can have different (and sometimes conflicting) interests, so sometimes, as a business owner you must make trade offs to please them all.

Understanding, managing, and balancing the needs of your stakeholders is critical to the success of your business.

Look at it this way—what might happen if you only cater to your customers and not your investors? The investors might pull funding, making it not only challenging but impossible for you to serve your customers.

Similarly, failing to consider your employees might mean high turnover rates and difficulty in creating synergy in your business practices.

As the branding process unfolds, research about stakeholders will inform a broad range of solutions, from positioning to the tilt of brand messages, to the launch strategy and plan.

Thus, it is important for you to identify, understand and research your key stakeholders with the help of a suitable agency and then cater to them appropriately.

Exercise

1. Map your internal customers.

2. Map your external customers.

Key Benefits of Strong Brand Culture

Branding is not an activity or exercise that you undertake in isolation as it's evident from the vast number of stakeholders who have invested in its outcome. It is something that should be ingrained top-down in the culture of your company and internalised by your staff so that it becomes the standard method of doing business for everyone.

Long-term success is directly influenced by the way the employees share in their company's culture—its values, story, symbol, and heroes. It is only possible to build your brand sustainably from the inside-out when the employees (your internal customers/ stakeholders) share in and embrace your brand's purpose.

How strongly people believe in an organization and its basic precepts defines the strength of its success.

Brand Culture doesn't always permeate (what are you trying to tell) the organization through the visible organization structure,

instead it flows through the organization via the invisible community connections that are an inevitable part of every organization. The invisible community proves very effective in transmitting the brand culture.

THE VISIBLE ORGANIZATION	THE INVISIBLE COMMUNITY
Hierarchy & Chain of Command	Network of Reliable Relationships
Official Values & Vision	Experienced Values & Vision
Written Rules, Policies & Procedures	Unwritten Rules & Social Norms
Business Contracts (Internal & External)	Informal Contracts (Internal & External)
Business Accountabilities	Social Accountabilities
Information/Communication Systems	The Back Channel (Grapevine/Rumor Mill)

***Image & Chart Courtesy: Hanley Brite, Founder, Authentic Connections**

Let me share with you the key benefits of a strong brand culture

1. Delighted Customers

Customers are attracted to brands where the brand culture is evident through formal branding as well as through the commitment and behaviour of their employees.

2. Natural Brand Ambassadors

A strong brand culture fosters committed and passionate employees who believe in the organization and act as your brand ambassadors when they are out in the world, thus creating more brand awareness than any advertising campaign ever could. In addition to your employees, your customers could also be your natural brand ambassadors, because what works better than word of mouth.

3. Higher Productivity

Engaged and happy employees are always more productive, leading to more profitability and therefore, more success.

4. Standing Out From the Competition

Companies with a strong brand culture can create a clear differentiation and stand head & shoulders above their competition through their customer relationships, higher productivity and informal brand engagement due to employees aligned with the company's purpose.

5. Attracting & Retaining Talent With Ease

Organizations with a strong brand culture obviously have a great work environment and opportunities for growth since their employees are aligned with their vision and enjoy working there. Hence it is easy for them to attract & retain talent whether as employees, partners, consultants or vendors.

6. Better Interpersonal Dynamics

A strong brand culture gives people common, shared goals and thus makes collaborations and working on cross-functional teams smoother and speedier.

Thus, fostering a strong brand culture under the guidance of an experienced and insightful agency is essential. Brand culture is the glue that holds your organization together. It is the core of your organization, like a person's DNA.

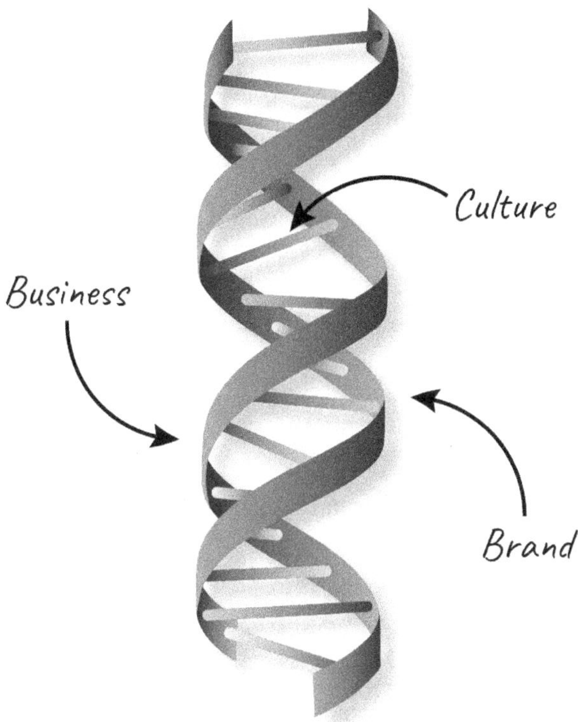

The Emotional Branding Concept

"Customers define themselves through brands they use. The branded clothes they wear, the cars they drive, the drinks they consume, the university they attend, favourite spots to hang out, and so on."

Marc Gobé created the concept of emotional branding over 15 years ago. His philosophy is based on the observation that connections can take place on an emotional level in relationships between brands and people.

Consumers associate with brands they feel reflect their identity and when a close emotional link to a brand is formed emotions can run high – for example people who like Pepsi usually despise Coke!

Successful Practitioners of Emotional Branding

Pepsi, Oil of Olay and Mercedes are a few major brands requiring little introduction. Their appeal ranges from youthfulness to status, but these brands share a deep emotional connection with their customers which translates into unwavering consumer loyalty.

Apple is another brand illustrating the effectiveness of emotional branding. Apple almost went under in the 1990's but an amazing brand rejuvenation propelled it to the 21st century super-brand status.

Wired.com reported Gobe's saying—Apple has succeeded in giving its product a humanized touch in an ever-evolving technical world. Responding to consumer anxiety about technology's evolutionary speed, Apple managed to make its customers feel like a part of the brand by making it clear that the brand understands their needs.

Brands like Bing and Google are also adopting an emotional brand-driven approach. Recent Google commercials show people talking about average things and emotionally connecting through Gmail.

Bing Originals' new campaign brings celebrities down to consumer level; winning, falling, healing. People can feel bonded with these brands when the brands demonstrate they understand their consumers' needs and motivations.

The recent rejection of Twitter by many users due to Elon Musk's inhumane behaviour with his employees is a classic example of consumer behaviour being driven by emotions.

Putting Customers First

So, what is it that you can do to show and communicate that the customer is your top priority above all other considerations?

The foremost thing is to decide which emotion it is that you are looking to target and tap into in your potential audience. Identifying, understanding, and defining your market's core emotional need is crucial to building a successful emotional connect with your audience. This is the key to effective emotional branding. Once identified, it is vital that all your communication whether internal or external be aligned to their emotional needs.

When your efforts are driven by considering what your customers need, want, and aspire to, you facilitate emotional bonding. This ultimately brings your customer to a stage where they say, "I will only buy brand x?"

The key is to keep your communications consistently focused on your customers' emotional needs. Each interaction whether it is through your customer relations team, your online content or your social media engagement should showcase and reiterate that the brand is sensitive to its customers' emotional needs.

A customer's emotional attachment to a brand is a bond similar to and as strong as an attachment that they may have to a person.

In such a scenario, the customer finds it hard to separate themselves from that particular brand and choose a new way to enter into a relationship with a new brand. It almost feels like cheating.

A charismatic brand can only be built through emotional branding and emotional branding can only be achieved by understanding the science and the key ingredients for developing a brand.

1.0
The five senses

Branding is the process of converting a prospect into a customer through an emotional connect.

A buying decision is 5% conscious and 95% unconscious; it's that grey area of the subconscious where branding influences the customer.

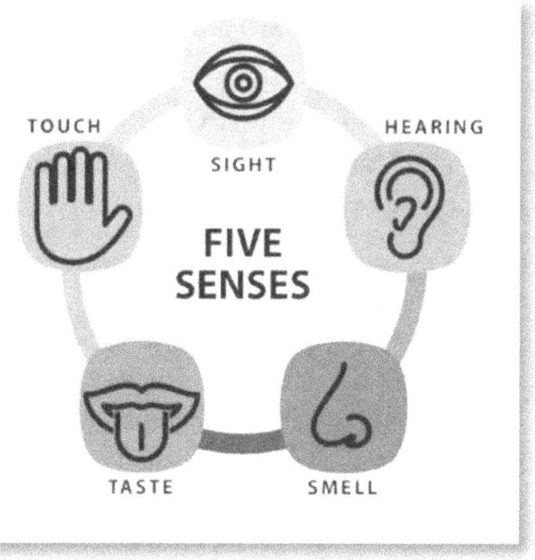

Our 5 senses and emotions are very tightly intertwined and subconsciously affect our decision making. Let me illustrate this through an example again.

This example tells us how important it is for a brand to engage the senses in order to connect with people's emotions and inspire trust and confidence so they choose you over the competition.

Building Trust Currency Via The Senses: The VISA Case Study

Even though we all live in a digital world today, if we were to be honest, I think most of us would admit that we are still skeptical about and scared of making online payments because they are automatic, non-personal and invisible. We are physically unable to see, hear and feel the payment being processed. **It is extremely challenging for payment service providers to inspire confidence in customers during an online payment transaction because so many of our senses are not engaged.**

However, Visa has achieved this feat through its Visa sensory branding suite, branding suite, which is a combination of sensory brand marks such as animation, sound, and haptic created for such environments on the web and mobiles.

The Visa brand has established an environment of trust, security and customer friendliness universally through various sensory cues [animation of the Visa brand mark (engaging your visual sense), the Visa sound (engaging your aural sense-sense of hearing), and the Visa haptic pattern synthesized into one timeline] designed to evoke the same emotions that a traditional Visa brand mark would evoke in you in a physical payment experience.

As is evident from the VISA case study above, The Visa brand makes the customer feel confident, secure, assured and safe when they pay using this platform because it engages their senses despite being online.

Another great thing about the Visa branding suite is how they have conveyed and reinforced their desired message through the sensory experience.

They have deliberately kept the duration of their sensory cues short by design because they wanted to portray an image perception of speed and convenience- that using Visa is quick and hassle-free.

A brand is not just a logo or a product, or a service. It is an experience that touches the senses!

Moving this conversation forward, I'd like you to meet an old friend of mine.

This friend worked hard and dominated the radio world for 42 years, from 1952 to 1994, serenading people's emotions through his baritone voice coupled with Bollywood's choicest melodies.

A Dear Old Friend

Meet my dear old friend Ameen Sayani, who not only established himself as a personal brand but was also turned instrumental in helping Binaca (later named Cibaca & back to Binaca again) toothpaste that hogged the market share ruthlessly, killing all competitions for years.

So why were Binaca & Ameen Sayani successful? Well, of course, the reason was that they connected with people's emotions, as we know, is essential to success.

But the big question is how did they connect to people's emotions?

As we have already discussed, a brand is a sensory experience that the consumer associates with the company/product/service.

Cibaca managed to touch and capture the three major senses of its consumers.

It catered to their visual sense through its distinctive logo and innovative visual campaigns.

Perhaps, we can add an image of one of their campaigns

It catered to their sense of taste through its unique taste that was different from the other kinds of toothpaste in the market.

And finally, it catered to their sense of hearing (auditory sense) in one of the most innovative ways through sponsoring a radio music show, the weekly Binaca *Geetmala* hosted by the inimitable Ameen Sayani.

This show literally imprinted brand Binaca in people's minds, not because it was the only choice or absolutely the best choice, but because it connected with their emotions and played on their senses. And this is why for years, other toothpaste brands like Colgate, Closeup, etc, could only muster a meager 2-3% of the market share while Binaca lorded it over with the lion's share.

And remember, any company/product/service that connects to three or more of the consumer's senses will imprint itself on their psyche and be their first choice.

Enhance your Brand by Capturing the Senses

Using a suite of sensory branding cues is beneficial and enhances your customers' experience.

In consumer research, 81% of users said they would have a more positive perception of merchants who use either sound or animation cues for branding.

Let me share another great and unique example with you that illustrates branding through the olfactory senses.

Aromatherapy by Singapore Airlines: Sensual Branding

To boost its corporate identity in 1990, Singapore Airlines came up with a unique way to leave an imprint on its customers' senses. To begin with, they commissioned Stefan Floridian waters that had a typically warm and welcoming aroma. And then, they decided to make this aroma the core of their entire customer experience.

Comforting the olfactory senses of the passengers, a new set of brand tools was developed by the airlines in the AROMA.

The aroma specially designed for Singapore airlines is now a signature of everything related to the airlines.

Be it the perfume their hostesses wear, the way their newspapers smell, the aroma inside the aircraft, or even the smell emanating from the hot towels given to passengers just before the flight takes off.

This aroma permeates the entire service scape and assails the customers' senses pleasurably.

This aroma has now become a distinctive trademark of Singapore Airlines.

This aroma serves as a warm, comfortable memory even after passengers disembark, and this makes them choose the airlines over and over again. Thus, I am sure my entrepreneur friends understand the need and importance of sensory engagement in effective branding.

12 Emotions –

Joy, Sorrow, Anger, Fear, Surprise, Disgust, Anxiety, Love, Guilt, Shame, Pride, and Pain

EMOTION is the only thing that's common in all.

"Emotional branding is a dynamic cocktail of anthropology, imagination, sensory experiences, and visionary approach."

Exercise

1. So, how many senses does your brand touch?

____

____

____

____

____

____

____

____

____

2. What can you do to develop extra sense for your brand?

____

____

____

____

____

____

____

____

*"A good brand is nothing
more than trust."*

2.0

Colours Play

Okay riddle me this: why do you think no one feels like lounging around in a McDonald's whereas one can sit comfortably in Starbucks for hours? The answer might shock you—it's because of the design and colour play.

Red, blue, orange, green, purple, magenta, black and white, whatever is the colour, each of these colours have a psychological impact on what we think and how we feel that's why choosing the colour for your brand should never be based on your personal preference or aesthetic taste but a strategic decision to shape your brand's image.

Therefore, it is important to learn to use colour psychology in branding and marketing so you can understand the psychological impact of colour on decisions and emotions.

You can influence how your customers perceive your brand using colours.

Since people develop an emotional connection to colours from early childhood. The right colour can make people feel calm, happy, or vibrant. The wrong colour can invoke feelings of fear, danger, or even oppression.

This understanding of the psychology of colours makes choosing your brand colours all the more important. It is essential to consider colour meanings before committing to your brand's colour scheme.

Here, I am sharing with you some popular colours and their connotations briefly

Code RED

Red creates a sense of urgency making it really effective for sales & CTA buttons. It also encourages appetite—McDonald's has used it effectively. Speaking of red, the interiors of 'McDonald's' is scientific. The red colour is an energizing hue that represents activity and stimulates appetite. However, the red also asks you to order and take away the food, therefore, literally asking to "Fuck off".

Red also evokes a feeling of excitement which is why fast cars and lingerie are really popular in red.

One of the most famous brands in the world, Coca-Cola uses the colour red to create a sense of appetite, excitement, and an urge to have it right now!

Netflix & Levi's are also great examples of the scientific use of the colour red.

The Youthfulness of Yellow

Yellow represents youthfulness, happiness, fun, and sunshine and it denotes optimism, warmth, happiness, creativity, intellect, and extroversion.

Some household name brands that use the color yellow include McDonald's, Hertz, post-it, DHL, IMDb, Nikon, Yellow Pages, Shell, and the Commonwealth Bank.

Going Green!

In the last decade or so, green has been a little bit overused with eco-friendly branding and the concept of going green.

Green is more than just about eco-friendliness, it also represents power and we see it in finances and the military.

Famous brands using green are British Petroleum, Energy Australia, Animal Planet, Whole Foods, Land Rover, Starbucks, etc.

Orange Bright Orange

Orange like yellow and red is a warm and vibrant color. Its brightness inspires innovation, excitement, and confidence.

Also, orange is often used to denote affordability and accessibility by brands such as

Amazon, MasterCard, Continental Hermes, Firefox, EasyJet, Nickelodeon, Penguin books, etc.

Black to the Basics

The color black is elegant and sophisticated with connotations of wealth and class and so it is abundantly used in many luxury brands from Chanel to Prada and Gucci. So when you consider using black in branding use it strategically.

Brands using the colour black include Nike, Chanel, WWF, Hugo Boss, Jack

Daniels, Puma, and Ralph Lauren.

White is Right!

White is associated with purity, cleanliness, simplicity, and innocence.

Brands that use the colour white include Adidas, Cartier, Lexus, Prada, Sony, Tesla, and Zara.

Obviously, there are many different ways to communicate your brand to your target audience but choosing the best colour for your brand is a crucial tool.

The first step in any marketing and branding decision is understanding your target audience.

You should know who you are trying to influence, and who your brand exists to serve—know who these people are, you need to know their likes, their dislikes, their hopes, their dreams, and biggest fears and understand their market demographics and their psychographics.

This will help you make ongoing strategic decisions regarding the colours to use in your branding.

While it is really important to choose colours that feel appropriate to your industry and authentic to your products and services, it is also important to remember that you need to stand out from the competition and differentiate yourself from the rest of the market.

Therefore, you will need to work with colours that strike a balance between your industry as well as your unique brand identity and strategy.

Colours evoke emotions and when you understand the attributes that your audience is attracted to, the role that you want to play in their lives, and the message you want to send them, then your colour can play a really important role in shaping how they perceive your brand.

It is critical that you find the right combination of colours to psychologically convince your audience to emotionally invest in your business since emotion often drives purchasing decisions.

Task: So what are the colours that represent your brand?

Exercise

1. Can you build a colour story for your brand? And how?

"Brands continue to exist because they constantly narrate stories."

3.0

Deriving your Brand Persona

There are multiple models available to decipher your Brand Persona. Here I am demonstrating one commonly used technique.

Brand Archetypes

Archetypes are essentially twelve personality types that everyone has a collective understanding of, though we may not be conscious of it. Basically, we have this inherent understanding of these types of behaviours and we are able to recognize them when we see them.

We see these archetypes as individual characters that we interact with in our lives in person, or as characters in literature and media. As I said earlier, you will instinctively recognize these characteristics when you see those behaviours exhibited.

Now you might be wondering why we should be talking about and trying to understand these archetypes. Well, simple answer—these archetypes apply to brands too. And understanding these archetypes will help you position and build your brand as per the personality type/archetype of your target customer.

Let's explore these in detail.

The Outlaw Archetype

The outlaw archetype is a personality type that we all recognize. Though they often get into trouble, the outlaw is not all negative, the common outlaw has this burning desire for freedom, and for liberation and for change.

If we were to understand this in terms of branding an apt example would be Harley Davidson.

The Magician Archetype

The magician archetype a desire for power alongside an aura of secrecy and mystery. When it comes to brands, Disney is probably the most magical brand and it really uses the magician archetype throughout its brand communication.

The Hero Archetype

The hero archetype has a burning desire to win and to save the day. The hero is typically determined, courageous, aggressive, competitive and they really want to win.

When it comes to brands no one epitomizes the hero more than Nike, it celebrates heroes throughout its advertising, whether that's Serena Williams or Tiger Woods, it really puts the heroes on a pedestal. The modern-day heroes today are athletes and that's what it does celebrating these athletes as heroes.

The Lover Archetype

The lover archetype has a burning desire for intimacy.

The lover archetype tends to be sensual exotic, sensitive, affectionate, and almost always sexy. When it comes to branding, a good lover archetype would be Victoria's Secret obviously because of the sensuality and the seductiveness involved with that brand.

The Jester Archetype

The jester has a desire for laughter. The jester tends to be full of humour, positivity and excitement and this character is widespread across cinema, pick up any comedy movie and the star is a jester.

When it comes to branding, the Old Spice brand has really taken on that jester archetype and personality.

It wasn't always that way, it only happened in the 90s when it was seen as this kind of middle-of-the-road, middle-aged brand and it really took this new direction and brought the Jester archetype into its brand strategy and started appealing to the younger generation. The part of its overall strategy now is to make its audience laugh and to give them a sense of enjoyment.

The Everyman Archetype

The everyman archetype wants nothing more than to fit in, just wants to belong. They just want to be normal, they don't want to stand out, they don't want to be in the limelight and they just want to be accepted.

They just want to feel like they belong, the everyman type tends to be humble, welcoming, and friendly. When it comes to branding, IKEA is a great example of an everyman brand and they even have it in their tagline. What it's saying there is that we're for everybody and we're not pretentious and if you want to belong, if you want to be one of us, if you just want to be normal then we have the furniture for you.

The Caregiver Archetype

The caregivercare giver archetype has a desire to give service.

The character of this archetype tends to be kind, warm, loving, caring. Great examples of a caregiver brand would be WWF or UNICEF.

The Ruler Archetype

The ruler archetype is all about control, they have this desire to control and to impose their authority.

When it comes to brands, pretty much any high street brand here is using some kind of ruler archetype because what they're appealing to that level of status so a very good example of the ruler archetype in branding would be Mercedes.

The Creator Archetype

The creator archetype is all about innovation and imagination.

The creator archetype tends to see things that other people don't because they think outside the box they tend to have grand visions, innovation and imagination.

When it comes to brands, one of the most famous creator archetype brands would be Apple because it has aligned itself with the idea that people who think differently can change the world.

The Innocent Archetype

The innocent archetype has a desire for safety.

Any brand that embraces natural things or organic things or things the way nature intended would be seen as an innocent brand so great examples here would be vino or the body shop who really embraced sustainability, are excellent examples of brands that embrace natural or organic things and hence, the innocent archetype works well in their favour.

The Sage Archetype

The sage archetype has this desire for knowledge and wisdom so anyone who is really there to help and guide you in the right direction could be seen as the sage. They also have a desire to share that knowledge and help people.

A wise brand might be any company that offers guidance and solutions; Google is the ideal illustration of this. Any brand that provides answers and provides the way forward could be seen as a sage brand, so a perfect example of that would be Google.

The Explorer Archetype

The explorer archetype has a desire for adventure.

They have to try new things all the time and challenge themselves to do something different.

In the branding world, any brand that really kind of explores the outdoors, celebrates the outdoors or provides tools to go out and celebrate the outdoors would be considered an explorer archetype, so an example here would be Patagonia or Jeep.

I've no doubt that when you saw all of those archetypes you felt more attracted to one or two than the rest and there's a reason for this it's because your personality makes you more attracted to those characteristics and regardless of which characteristic you're attracted to, you will have certainly recognized each and every one of those because they're in your innate understanding of other people's behaviours and that's called your collective unconscious.

This is why, they're so effective when it comes to building strategic brands because brands today connect with their customers through personality, through human connection and through emotion so you definitely need to understand brand archetypes and implement them in formulating your brand strategy.

Archetypes	Enables people to	Follower Brand
Creator	Make something new	DLF
Caregiver	Care for others	Himalaya
Ruler	Take control	Relience
Jester	Have fun	Radio Mirchi
Regular guy/ orphan	Be ok as themselves	Big Bazaar
Lover	Find and give love	Nykaa
Hero	Be brave	Bullet Motocycle
Outlaw/ Destroyer	Break the rules	Thumsup
Magician	Bring about transformation	Tata
Innocent	Retain or renew faith	Mother Dairy
Explorer/ Seeker	Maintain independence	ONGC
Sage	Understand their world	Patanjali

Exercise

1. Which of these Archetypes do you thnik your brand fits in?

*"Believe in strategic endeavour.
It works wonders."*

Chapter - Seven

Your saarthi

Your Guiding Charioteer

Ok folks its story time, grab your mugs of tea/coffee and lend me your ears (Lol eyes in this case, since you are reading this) but hey! I am engaging all your senses.

Saarthi: A Story of Grace & Guidance

When the *Pandavas* had won the war of *Mahabharata* and were returning back home from the victory, *Arjuna* was full of pride after defeating *Duryodhana* and his entire army.

He felt that he was the strongest of all warriors and it was he who had defeated the entire army as he had the best archery skills. He was filled with immense pride at his achievement. On returning to the camp, when the chariot came to a standstill, *Krishna* asked *Arjuna* to get down from the chariot first. What with his bloated victory ego, this didn't go down well with *Arjuna*. He said you are the *Saarthi* (the charioteer) so you get down first and then I will get down.

Krishna requested again that, friend you please get down and then I will get down. This led to an argument about who should get down first, while this was going on, *Dharmraj Yudhishthira's* chariot slid up to them. When he overheard the argument he told *Arjuna* that since *Lord Krishna* is saying something then there must be some valid reason behind it and he should get down.

Though *Arjuna* was not happy still he got down reluctantly from the chariot. After he and the others were at a safe distance from the chariots, *Lord Krishna* got down from the chariot and the moment he moved away from it, there was a huge explosion in *Arjuna's* chariot and it was torn apart by the force of the explosion and broke down into small pieces.

Arjuna and all the others were astonished and could not believe what they saw.

Though he understood why *Krishna* had asked him to get down from his chariot first he did not understand what was going on.

So with folded hands he walked towards *Lord Krishna* and asked him what was this magic all about?

With a smile *Lord Krishna* replied that during the war there were multiple attacks on you with dangerous, powerful weapons. This chariot protected you from all of them since I was your charioteer and my grace was working as a shield and I was guiding you in the right direction. And that is why all those weapons did not harm you.

Had I got down first today then even after winning the battle on the field, you would have lost the battle of life unprotected in that chariot. In that moment, *Arjuna* realized that what he had been thinking of as his victory all this time was in reality Lord Krishna protecting him. Hold your horses, you're all thinking why am I telling you this story?

This story from Mahabharata is my unique way of explaining one of the key concepts of brand growth in simple terms.

And this key concept is your *Saarthi*, your Charioteer.

Earlier we have talked about your business being a chariot pulled in opposite directions by the horses that should ideally be driving it to its destination (success).

So this is where the need for a charioteer comes in.

In *Mahabharata,* it was *Krishna* who donned the role of sovereignty. He was the *Saarthi,* and that too of the most powerful and the best archer in the entire world was *Arjuna*.

Krishna was the advisor in the Mahabharata. That brand advisor or the growth advisor who took the seat of the *Saarthi* during the time of actual war.

He was not merely the charioteer of the physical chariot in the war but also the guiding mentor & advisor in off the battlefield.

During the course of the *Mahabharata,* apart from the sermons which he gave to *Arjuna,* his role was manifold—the understandings and the growth path which he set for him, guiding him when to stop and when to start, advising him on what he should do and what he should not do, even what he should think and what he should not.

He played a key role in the *Mahabharata.* And that's precisely what a true advisors role is. A true advisor is nothing but a *Saarthi* to your business, a capable entity who holds your powerhouses and gives them a direction.

Who keeps their eyes and ears open for any external enemies erupting that could harm you. They are the one who will shield you in your journey to success. The one who tells you what you should do and what you should not. Who guides you when you should attack the market and when you should lie low!

And they do it not for their benefit, not for their growth, but to make sure that you be victorious in every business battle.

This story is applicable in the current business scenario too. It is important to remember that behind your success there are so many *Krishnas* who have held your hand and guided you during adversities, who shielded you from all attacks and helped you navigate your business journey.

Mapping the *Mahabharata* our current business scenarios, we can see that the promoter is the driving force, the consumers are the horses and the external environment where the war is being waged is your enemy.

It is very important to understand your enemy which is the competition and deeply impacts your business. It is just not enough to keep an eye rather it is important to keep an eye on all the movements the market is making. The most important being the consumer, their changing habits and the social & cultural changes. This understanding of consumer insights is critical and this can only be done by professionals, who understand the integrity and vital importance of this.

The ways of the modern consumer have changed which is impacting what it takes for brands to win.

The consumer in today's world is exposed to more than 6000 brand messages per day far too many for their brains to handle.

Consumers are constantly distracted while working, walking, texting, searching, eating – rarely doing one thing at a time.

Consumers are tired of being burned by faulty brand promises.

Their instinct is doubt first, test second, and at any point they are ready to trash the brands that do not live up to their expectation.

However, they remain loyal to the brands that speak directly to them, those that offer amazing experiences and those that exceed their expectations.

In the present scenario, consumers are taking control of the buying process. They have all info on their fingertips and they feel empowered with the influence they bring. But despite all this the thing to remember here is that consumers may explore rationally but will engage emotionally with the brands they trust.

In the present scenario, branding/advertising agencies play a key role in facilitating brand success.

Branding is a huge investment; I don't mean just money here, it not only requires time and risk but it also involves a lot of emotional investment as well.

That's why choosing the right branding agency is of utmost importance. Nothing could be worse than going through the rigorous process of building your brand and then having to start from scratch again only because you chose the wrong partner.

The agency needs to be perfectly aligned with organization. Having been a part of advertising agencies for more than two decades and having worked with multiple brands across multiple categories and nations, I have observed that there are typically three types/categories of agencies.

- Purpose Driven Agencies,

- Creative Agencies, and

- Growth Driven Agencies

First, there are purpose driven agencies which are much more focused. There are very few agencies providing these services, but there are many consultancy agencies which develop the purpose for an organization and deliver long term strategy to the client.

They develop a complete road map for the next five years and suggest strategic growth areas and initiatives that need to be taken; however they play only a specific role for a limited time period. Once the deliverables and modes of delivery are discussed and completed, they disappear.

Since they come really expensive, it is tough to hold onto them for long. However, if the organization religiously follows and builds upon the insights they deliver then they are likely to become unchallengeable brands.

They define the brand strategy which is effective in providing a central, unifying idea around which all behaviour, actions and communication is aligned. It works across all the products and services and is effective over time.

The effective strategies are so differentiated and powerful that they deflect the competition.

They are easy to talk with whether you are a CEO or an employee. **They align the vision, action**, expression, and **the experience**. They develop the brand architecture that will be the guiding factor for the parent company, subsidiary companies, products and services mirroring the marketing strategy which help the company to scale and market themselves effectively.

These companies use multiple tools, discussions with the leadership team, researching the market to gather consumer insights, developing the brand soul which leads to the development of a big idea. The big idea guides everything that the consumer touches.

A winning brand concept comes through consumer insights which is

1   Emotional benefits – How do they make them feel?

2   Functional benefits – What do consumers get?

3   Product features – What does your product do?

4   Targets & insights – What do consumers want?

Typically, these are the roles of the strategic teams to develop many agencies and have planners who look into this.

Either the strategic teams develop these guidelines and give them to the management to oversee. Or they hand them over to their creative agencies to look into but these things keep changing since the needs of the new age consumer keep changing constantly and they need to match with their expectations.

Then there are Creative led agencies that focus on producing outstanding creatives. They have a full-fledged team of art and copy supported by an entire ecosystem.

They have great understanding of the consumer insights and are experienced enough to deliver outstanding work. They know how to flirt with the consumer playing with emotional and functional benefits.

They have an understanding of colour play with the five senses to deliver outstanding campaigns whether it is print, TV or digital. These are teams who win awards and take organizations to the next level.

These are companies who follow Brand Guidelines or even help in developing Brand Guidelines with their planners. They deep dive into the customers' needs and pains to develop the big idea for the consumer to talk about.

Then there are Growth led agencies. They are more sales led and are specialized agencies providing specialization which could be E-mail marketing, YouTube, Instagram, events, media, outdoor or any specialized areas giving instant gratification in terms of sales.

These are technologically driven and have a strong inventory of various marketing products which they leverage giving instant results. However, these types of agencies are more of tactical agencies; they are neither strategic nor creative led. They may or may not focus on technology to deliver results, they are focused only on numbers. Their relation is transactional and they are least bothered with macro level thinking, they are busy with micro outputs without being bothered about the organizations' vision.

These agencies are in bulk across the country and these boutique agencies have built a specialized talent for the same however **it is really difficult to find a combination of an agency which delivers Purpose + Creative + Growth.**

Balance is the Key

The ideal combination for hiring an agency is one which has strategic and creative teams and in most company's strategy is separated from creative. Typically, agencies have **left brained people who are analytical, logical, linear, numerical or verbal; this breed of people or strategic thinkers. They understand numbers, they are firm believers of research and spend a considerable amount of their time in research.**

On the other hand there are **right brained people who are intuitive, emotional, and visual and they are creative thinkers.**

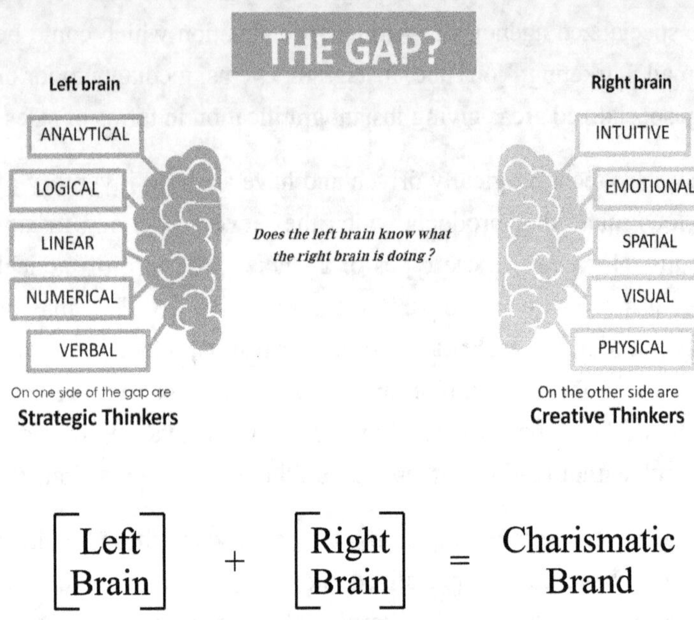

$$\begin{bmatrix} \text{Left} \\ \text{Brain} \end{bmatrix} + \begin{bmatrix} \text{Right} \\ \text{Brain} \end{bmatrix} = \text{Charismatic Brand}$$

And the problem starts when left brain does not know what right brain is thinking.

This is a big gap in all agencies, strategy and creative are not hand in glove or many a times clients provide the strategy but while executing they are not in sync.

"When both the strategic & creative sides work together you can build a Charismatic brand"

And we have already discussed earlier in detail that a Charismatic Brand is any product, service or organization for which people believe there is no substitute.

Having the right agency is critical for efficient and effective branding. The importance of having an agency with the right mix of right-brained and left-brained teams cannot be emphasized enough.

An agency that is a mix of right and left-brained resources will be able to work smoothly on the creative as well as the strategic aspects of *"**Brandvertising.**"*

It is often observed that most agencies are led by creative leads, such as creative directors or copy heads. As a result, in most cases, the creative people are driving and influencing the marketing decisions, which ought to be taken by strategic professionals on the marketing team.

Creative + Strategy = Successful Branding

People working on the account who are mainly creative often forget to understand the actual purpose of the brand. By not understanding the purpose, they are actually damaging the brand instead of building it.

The sad part is that in most cases, even the client is not clear about the brand's purpose. They themselves don't know what the brand stands for and why does it exist? They are busy in sales and marketing doing unstructured work, which keeps them occupied for no reason and yields no fruitful results.

Thus to choose the right agency, you must first understand the needs of your own business, as shared in the previous chapters and then ensure that your agency is a mix of creative and strategic skill sets, and the creative and strategic teams should work in sync so that the brand identity and voice are not compromised and remain consistent always. Only then will they impact the customer. Otherwise, all your money and effort will be wasted

So what is a Brandvertising Agency?

A firm that specializes in the strategic and creative work that shapes a business' identity, especially how it is perceived by internal and external stakeholders, is called a Brandvertising agency.

It is the *Saarthi, critical* to your brand's success like *Krishna* was to Arjuna's victory in the Mahabharata.

Chapter Eight

The future of branding

Even the smallest things can teach you valuable lessons about life. Let me share a story with you. So, it's a story of how bumblebees are not aware of the real and actual purpose. Bumblebees travel to flowers every morning to collect nectar and bring it back to their honeycombs. However, these bees are unaware that cross-pollination is actually their primary objective. Cross-pollination occurs as they carry the sticky nectar from flowers, which causes the seeds to attach to their bodies and fall off when they sit on another bloom. As a result, bumblebees help in the proliferation of plants.

Similarly, the goal of mankind is not only to accumulate wealth and gain profit. Our goal is also to raise the standard of living for all other people. So, let's build a revolutionary future of branding together.

It's time to be out there *for the world.*

The only *Dharma* of an entrepreneur is being purpose-driven.

In the era of existential crisis, even for brands, purpose can give your business the right spirit it needs to stay relevant, strive, and thrive. I am not referring to materialistic purposes here. It's bigger. It's spiritual. It's humane. The purpose that gives meaning to your brand and drives you to create a better society for everyone around.

Apparently, Marc Benioff had it all at the age of 34. Well, why wouldn't he? He started as a software executive at Oracle, a major provider of database software, and rose through the ranks to become its youngest vice president at the age of 26 and accumulated enormous riches.

However, by 1996, he was exhausted and thus, took a break from Oracle. He, along with a friend, travelled to India for two months.

They both happened to come across a spiritual *guru.* Benioff described his private meeting with *Amma,* the *guru,* and how it changed his life forever. So, he and his friend were explaining their business goals to Amma and how they were both going through an existential crisis. Amma looked at them and said, "In your quest to make money and succeed, don't forget to do something for others." This very thought stuck with Benioff.

Benioff founded Salesforce in 1999 after quitting Oracle. In response to Amma's words of wisdom, he set aside 1% of the stock to be used in the future to help others in need. With its trademark program, the **Pledge 1%**, Salesforce pledges to donate 1% of its profits and 1% of its goods to societal interests. The company made sure to work towards the betterment of society in more ways than simply money and kind by allocating

1% of its employees' time. Since its inception, over 10,000 businesses worldwide have joined the program. The outcome gives employees a sense of accomplishment. Moreover, the act dramatically improved Salesforce's reputation.

For a brand to exist, it needs a higher purpose. A purpose that's bigger than earning money or profits. A purpose that ensures sustainability. Because your brand needs widespread recognition, develop recognizable narratives and sell your distinctive charms and qualities. Allow your target audience to adore and respect you inexplicably. With the example of Marc Benioff, I think I have made my argument about how an objective (beyond financial rewards) may settle existential concerns and knit the entire globe into a single thread of social interest.

This, I foresee, is the very 'Future of Branding.'

Presenting to you story of based on true scenario

Let me tell you a tale about my friend Rajkumar Aggarwal, who mentored and guided me into the industry. While we were fighting for our careers in the late 1990s, he was operating his electrical trading firm and I was getting into advertising. While he was busy with his company, he always made time to volunteer at hospitals, organise Chabeel (milk water distribution), and Langgar (food for needy), organise pilgimages to religious sites for friends, clients, and relatives, as well as actively participating in various NGOs. But little did he realise that people were appreciating him and joining his humanitarian cause.

In managerial terms, he began by forming a tribe, which grew so large that, with the help of the government and the tribe, he was able to establish a school for special children. After seeing the effectiveness of this over a few years, he created a hospital that is affordable to the general public.

There are several people around us who are doing such wonderful things for society. They are not only renowned names in the industry, but they are also operating thriving enterprises. Their businesses no longer require a visiting card or a PowerPoint presentation. Their reputation takes precedence over their business. Many business houses have clearly realised this and are focused on the job they perform, for example, the Azim Premji Foundation's concentration is on education.

No one can even consider coming close to the trust that TATAs have built. TATA is one such prominent illustration. Due to the company's well-known work and efforts on social causes, both customers and employees have long associated it with trust. Every entrepreneur should strive to create and maintain a brand of this calibre.

Since our enterprises cannot only be about making money, they must encompass a more comprehensive and profound meaning.

Today, to survive in the maddening market scenario, organisations that have been able to successfully develop their higher purpose they also need to amplify this so as to remain relevant in the market with the advent of numerous technologies it becomes much easier for them to exist.

"Companies that stand out are companies that stand out for something. These are the companies that customers and employees around the world would like to engage with."

Brand purpose enabled with technology can help a small entrepreneur think and build like large corporations.

With the changing times, with global warming, climate change, and the totally new way of living and doing business post pandemic, it has become essential that your brand purpose not be just self-centered.

In the new-age business world your purpose needs to be socially responsible too.

To have a magnetic brand purpose, it is important to be cognizant of the bigger socio-cultural movements and shifts because that is what makes the brand significant in the life of the consumer.

All brands solve a category problem, some better, faster, more effectively than others, but few brands transcend that and start becoming indispensable in the life of the consumer. Brands manage that when they are either culture current or culture activists. This allows them to have a definite brand purpose that impacts community.

It is this Culture Currency that allows brands like:

- **Apple** to be the creative catalyst in a person's life rather than just a computer that works better

- **Nike** to become a rallying cry for anyone who wants to push themselves to new heights rather than a running/jogging/ sports shoe

- **Maggi** to become a staple that someone grows up with and not just a 2 minute noodle

But how do we integrate a particular social program into our business?

Purpose supported with technology.

The "future of purpose-driven branding" thus includes efforts to address societal challenges such as climate change, resource conservation, inequality, and improving health and well-being of the affected society and then amplifying them to create social and business impact through technology.

"The future of branding is the seamless integration of the brand purpose and technology!"

From the author

The beginining of a change starts with the employee and the tools you give them

Develop your code of conduct

After discussing the future of branding as well as a larger purpose and objective for your organization, the final step is to treat it like a shrine. If you worship your work, everyone else will follow.

At this juncture, I have a vital question for you; how do you behave when you visit a spiritual or religious place or gathering? Think about it. Do you behave randomly in any way you wish, or do you follow an unspoken code of conduct? Do you walk into a temple with your shoes on? Do you talk loudly and gossip in a church or a gurdwara?

I'm confident that you will all respond "NO" in unison.

Temple is a place of worship, whether it's a small temple in your house, or outside. The rituals you follow haven't been provided to you in any form of text book but what you have learned from you parents and elders. Similarly, people of different age groups, sex, culture will be coming to your business and so, it is the entrepreneur's sole responsibility to maintain the sanctity of his business, sop that others follow throughout.

It's crucial for you to comprehend that following a business code of conduct is necessary for professional success. This basically means that you have to adhere to particular moral, flexible, and socially conscious business practices. However, not only you, the business owner, but every person in your company needs to be aware of these norms and work cohesively across hierarchies. This one code of conduct will eventually control all of the ecosystem's components, including your brand's extensions.

Your brand's code of conduct will serve as a representation of your brand's overall identity and will tie all of your employees together under one set of rules.

This will serve as your brand's Bible and be your brand book. The book must be revered by every employee and serve as a guide for brand extensions.

Saluting all the silent achievers for the lifetime of hard work they have put into building their brands.

- Ajay Adlakha

SO, IS BRANDING EXPENSIVE ...

... NO, IT IS PRICELESS!

Notes

Notes

I

9 *Actionable laws of branding for all businesses*

A successful branding process is a sequence based on the concept of uniqueness. The objective of the law of branding is to create a belief in the mind of the consumer that there is no other product on the market similar to your product.

This essential law of branding plays an important role in converting a regular business into a successful brand.

1 Law of Specialization/Concentration

Your brand becomes stronger when you are able to narrow down the focus.

Companies are often busy expanding their range. When I talk to entrepreneurs, they proudly speak about the number of SKUs and their plans for adding more in the future, which to me is short term.

Line extension is definitely important but it also takes a lot of effort and money. And having too many SKUs can lead to scattered efforts that will spread you thin.

To develop a powerful Brand in the minds of consumers, you need to narrow your brand, not expand it.

Good things happen when you narrow rather than expand your business. When you dominate a category, you become extremely powerful. In order to dominate a category, you must contact your brand's focus.

2   Law of Quality

Quality is definitely important, but Brands are not built by only quality.

Everybody thinks they can market their product/service by saying that it is a high-quality product, but in reality, things are not always so obvious. If you fail to meet customers' expectations, they will start looking for alternatives.

Quality is very critical to satisfying your customers and retaining their loyalty so they continue to purchase from you in the future. Quality products make an important impact on long-term revenue and profitability. They also give you the authority to charge and maintain higher prices. The crucial ingredient in the success of any brand is being committed to delivering reliable products.

3   Law of Publicity

The birth of a brand is accomplished with publicity, not advertising.

Today brands are born, not made. A new brand must be capable of generating favorable publicity in the media and society or it won't have a chance in the marketplace. And how do you generate publicity? Being the first in the segment is the best way to generate publicity. In other words, try to be the first brand in a new category.

However, that may not be always possible and that is where you will need publicity, even more, to stand out despite not being the pioneer.

Most companies develop their branding strategies as if advertising were their primary communications aspect. They're totally wrong. The strategy should be firstly developed from a publicity point of view. Today, influencers play a critical role in developing strategies, and there are many brands that are developed with insights from consumers vis-a-vis influencers.

4   Law of Advertising

Advertising is the fuel for the brand to keep it running.

Advertising is a very powerful tool, not to build leadership and maintain the lead. It is needed to keep the consumer engaged and build recall for your Brand.

5   Law of Leadership

A leading brand should push the category, not the brand.

The most efficient/productive way of developing a Brand is creating a new category. In other words, narrowing the focus where nothing is present. This will help in segmenting and remaining consistent. Positioning a brand into multiple categories creates confusion in the consumer's mind.

You should always remember that spreading a brand across multiple categories often weakens a brand; therefore, pick a category and focus all your efforts on it.

6   Law of the Name

A Name that others cannot copy

The name of your Brand is what differentiates it from competitors. So (if you haven't chosen it yet), give some serious thought to the name that you choose for your brand, as this will play a huge role in its long-term success.

Your Brand name should be catchy and easy to pronounce. And of course, it should represent your Brand personality and image.

7   Law of Persistence

A brand is not built overnight. Success is measured in decades, not years.

Many brands mistakenly believe that in order to grow, they need to change. But doing so dilutes the brand identity. The efforts put over ages go in vain the moment brands invest in makeovers, not realizing that consumers recognize brands by their colour , taste or smell.

The moment there is change they assume it is fake and the sales go for a toss. However when companies invest in re-branding, then there are longer goals in mind and they ensure they make high-decibel noise so that the consumers are aware of the changes.

So persist with your efforts and be consistent in your Branding.

8   Law of Fellowship

If you wish to remain relevant then welcome other Brands.

When competition is more, it increases the noise level and tends to increase sales in the category. Competition also expands the category while allowing the Brands to stay focused.

Consumers respond to competition because the choice is seen as a major benefit. If there is no choice, consumers are suspicious. Consumer will not show interest in buying a brand if they don't have another brand to compare with.

Your Brand should welcome healthy competition. It always brings more customers into the category.

9   Law of the Company

Brands are Brands. Companies are Companies.

Nothing causes as much confusion in the process of branding as the proper use of a company name. The issue of how to use a company name is at the same time simple and complicated. It is simple because the laws are so transparent. This process is complicated because it does not follow the simple law of branding and finally ends up with a system that defies logic and results in endless Brand-versus-Company debates.

When you put together a company name with a brand name in a clear and consistent fashion, the brand name is the primary name and the company name is seen as the secondary name.

There are many overlaps and there are of course a few more laws, however, if you follow these 9 essential law of branding from scratch your success ratio will be high in brand building and you can build a big brand amongst consumers. It is not a short term process, persistence and continuity will make the difference. If you are looking for instant gratification, you will be disappointed and will be tempted to give up midway.

When you sow seeds in your garden, you dont expect flowers the very next day, do you?

The same applies to your branding. You will need to be patient with the results.

The only thing that matters is what the consumer thinks about your brand and how *they* perceive it to be.

Now that we are at the conclusion of our interaction through this book and you understand the criticality of branding right, I am sure there is still one question clamoring in your mind:

II

The Dharma of an Entrepreneur

From all that you have imbibed through our interaction, I am sure that you understand how you can work in collaboration with your *Saarthi* (agency) to live out your Dharma as an entrepreneur to win big at your business. I am sharing below with you the essential action points to guide you onto this path of your entrepreneurial *Dharma*:

1. Develop a social purpose that is different from a business purpose - the foundation of your organization

2. Develop a unique leadership style that is charismatic.

3. Develop a business code of conduct.

4. Define and communicate the vision and purpose of the business powerfully.

5. Think of your brand as a person so that you can create BRAND LOVE.

6. Understand the concept of brand valuation and learn to play.

7. Commit to a real differentiator.

8. Stay relevant to keep the customer happy. Step into the shoes of the customer. Be your own customer.

9. Find a space where you can win.

10. Use technology to amplify.

11. Create a brand manual and update it from time to time.

12. Train team on branding from time to time.

13. Don't get into controversies such as politics and religion. Your role is to unite not divide.

14. Invest in research.

15. Invest time with your partners (Advertising agencies, PR, BTL, and Digital agencies) , they are like legs and arms for your growth, don't make frequent changes.

16. Develop your business tribe that people will be proud of.

17. Embrace a higher business purpose.

18. Create functional and emotional benefits for your brand to develop trust.

19. Understand your enemy inside out. In a war 99% is preparation and 1% is execution.

20. Shift your focus from product-centricity to customer-centricity.

21. Develop business on data and emotions.

22. Business is all about focus - The focus test

     a. Who are you?

     b. What do you do?

     c. Why does it matter?

23. Develop a Brand Architecture.

24. Focus on a big idea and organize the business around it like Apple's big idea- Make technology so simple that everyone can be part of the future.

25. Create Superheroes

26. Keep auditing your brand health

27. Keep Energizing the brand

**The three most
important words in
differentiating your
brand:**

FOCUS

FOCUS

FOCUS

IV
Key branding Strategies

1. Brand Purpose

2. Brand Vision, Mission & Values

3. Brand Positioning

4. Brand Personality & Tonality

5. Brand Story or Legacy

6. Tagline

These key elements define the brand which your brand *saarthi* can help you develop with deep thinking and tools many a time brands require rebranding or repositioning which needs to be done with the help of professionals having deep understanding and experience.

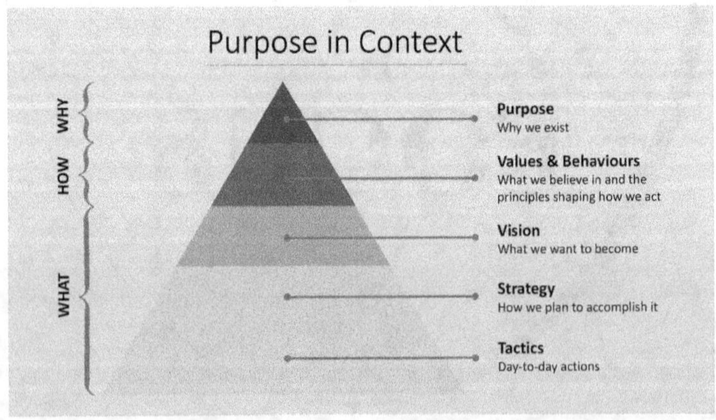

V
My upcoming training programs

1. Strategic Thinking

2. Briefing

3. Brand Positioning

4. Brand Analytics

5. Managing your Marketing Career

6. USA Framework - Unify, Simplify and Amplify

As the business, market, and technology have gotten more dynamic; it has become crucial to keep up with the trends to become trendsetters. Thinking, building, and growing has changed significantly. Hence, I have created specialized training programs for all entrepreneurs to educate them about the science of branding, establish customer-focused brands, design brand strategies, and assist you all to achieve the recognition and reach the success your businesses deserve.

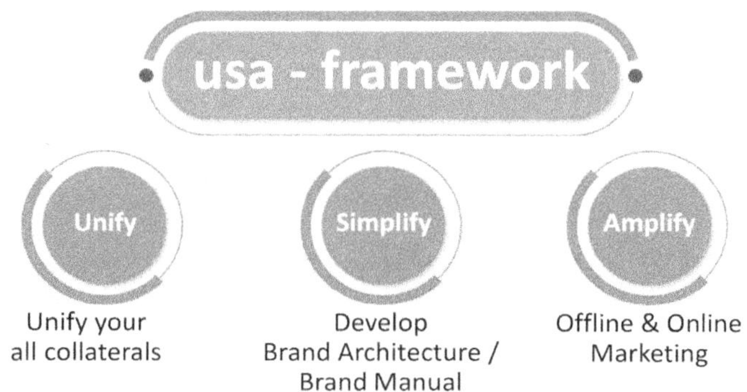

Disclaimer

The veracity of some articles may not be 100%, the author intends to explain the science of Marketing through these articles, in simple terms, for the aspiring entrepreneurs

9 789355 543158